Music Therapy for the Autistic Child

to Pussy with love

$ 17.60

Music Therapy
for the
Autistic Child

JULIETTE ALVIN

Second Edition by
AURIEL WARWICK

Oxford   New York
Oxford University Press

Oxford University Press, Great Clarendon Street, Oxford OX2 6DP

Oxford New York
Athens Auckland Bangkok Bogota Bombay
Buenos Aires Calcutta Cape Town Dar es Salaam
Delhi Florence Hong Kong Istanbul Karachi
Kuala Lumpur Madras Madrid Melbourne
Mexico City Nairobi Paris Singapore
Taipei Tokyo Toronto Warsaw

and associated companies in
Berlin Ibadan

Oxford is a trade mark of Oxford University Press

Published in the United States by
Oxford University Press Inc., New York

First edition published 1978
Second edition first published 1991
Second edition reprinted 1992, 1994, 1996, 1997

British Library Cataloguing in Publication Data
Data available

Library of Congress Cataloging in Publication Data
Music therapy for the autistic child.
Juliette Alvin.—2nd ed. by Auriel Warwick.
Includes bibliographical references.
1. Music therapy.   2. Autism.   I. Warwick, Auriel.   II. Title.
MT17.A48   1991   618.92'89206 5154—dc20   91–15963
ISBN 0-19-816276-6

Printed in Hong Kong

Contents

Preface to the second edition

Since the first edition of this book (1978), music therapy has broadened its horizons to include such diverse areas as work in the probation service and in the control of stress. There has been increasing recognition of its value, promoted largely by those music therapists who have undertaken research at Masters and Ph.D. levels. For some years, music therapists employed by the Health Service have had their own career and salary structure.

This could not have happened without the pioneering spirit of Juliette Alvin under whom I trained at the Guildhall School of Music and Drama in 1971. This second edition with additional descriptive case material is a dedication to her work. She is still remembered with affection by the original staff at the Chinnor Resource Unit for autistic children in Oxfordshire, one of the many units, centres and hospitals where she worked and where I have worked for two days a week since September 1984.

I have referred to this book on numerous occasions when preparing material for papers and workshops. It contains some fundamental truths expressed with empathy and compassion for the problems of the autistic child and the family. What Miss Alvin wrote during the mid-1970s is just as relevant today despite any changes in attitudes, philosophy and methodology. The second edition, therefore, includes all of the original text with three additional chapters (chh. 5–7) on new work.

We still know no definitive cause or causes for autism. There can be a genetic factor, the fragile X chromosomal disorder, which causes autistic features, but not all autistic children suffer from it. There was a period when the term 'autism' was used to explain any oddities of behaviour without enough careful diagnostic foundation, which would result only after close observation. Diagnosis is only the beginning. In my experience, after the diagnosis is made, too many parents and families are left to try to cope without any counselling and constructive help. They feel frightened, angry, bewildered and guilty. They have to go through a process of bereavement for the lack in their child of the ability to relate to others, combined with acute anxiety and fear of his or her environment. These children are often very attractive and, because they look normal, the general public is severe in its condemnation of parents who do not seem able to control the extreme behaviour of the child who screams in panic in the middle of a large and busy supermarket.

The final two chapters consist of case studies which describe not only what happened in the music therapy but also the early years before Sarah and Matthew started school and music therapy. From talking to parents of autistic children, I am sure that parents who read this book will identify with the problems encountered by Anne and Mark, and Helen and Simon, including the pain and frustration of trying to cope with the autistic child, the siblings and a ponderous, bureaucratic system.

Music therapy cannot cure such conditions as autism and mental handicap but it can alleviate the negative behaviours when the child is involved in interactive music-making with the therapist. So that the music therapist can meet the child on his or her own terms spontaneously, much of the music is improvised. The *Handbook of Terms* produced by the Association of Professional Music Therapists defines improvisation as 'any combination of sounds and silence spontaneously created within a framework of beginning and ending'. Clinical improvisation, as used in music therapy settings, is defined as 'musical improvisation with a specific therapeutic meaning and purpose in an environment facilitating response and interaction'. I have not worked with an autistic child who does not respond to musical sounds. This positive response has led to a popular misconception that autistic children have a talent for music. Some astonishing feats of musical perception and memory have been demonstrated by a few autistic people but in general they are not more or less musical than anyone else. One of the reasons for the attraction of music is that it bypasses language, which is a problem for most autistic people. Another is that music is a path to the world of feeling and emotion, a world which seems alien to the true autist. This book provides evidence that the power of music *can* reach the emotional world of the autistic child.

Finally, I would like to express my gratitude to the parents who have given permission for me to use case material. They have been generous and open in sharing their experiences and feelings in the hope that they might help other parents in similar situations.

Auriel Warwick

Introduction

All recently published books on autism mention one common feature present in autistic children, namely their response to music. This book is a comparative study in musical and autistic behaviour. It is an attempt to describe what long-term music therapy can achieve with some autistic children through skill, patience, understanding and love, and without unwarranted claims or ambitions.

The book is concerned with a number of autistic children under the care of medical and educational authorities in Great Britain. They belong to various social and ethnic backgrounds and have different clinical and family histories. They represent a fair sample of autistic types.

In spite of research the causes of autism are still unknown. Autism is a form of psychosis and consists of a number of well-known symptoms which may be present at different levels and in different degrees. They affect the mind, the body and the emotions of the child, but in many ways each autistic child is a unique individual, diagnosed under a label of a common syndrome.

Autism produces a state, or is a state, in which communication is gravely impaired, where normal relationship is distorted, defective or absent. The word 'relationship' should be taken here in its widest sense to include all the experiences through which a person matures physically, mentally and emotionally. It seems that some, but not always all, of the essential gradual steps leading to the growth of a human being are missing in the autistic child. Some of the links in the process of learning do not seem to exist. Therefore his behaviour is irrational, psychotic, and unpredictable. He often lives in a closed world of his own, not able or willing to communicate.

In music as in other fields, autism prevents the various factors which need to be integrated before success can be achieved from being put together. This happened with most of the cases described in the book. I did not hope to transform these children into good performers measured by conventional standards, but to offer each of them an integrated relationship through which he could mature and perhaps find a richer life.

I used the compelling power of sound to penetrate and to provoke in the child conscious or unconscious responses, hoping that music could not only reach him, but help him to reach out, in a two-way process of communication. I tried to make his responses become positive and purposeful in a non-threatening environment. The techniques aimed at creating all kinds of relationships between me and the child – between the child and the sounds – between the sounds of musical instruments and of his own voice. I hoped to develop and integrate through a musical experience his auditory, visual and tactile perception as well as his motor-control and use of space. The whole experience aimed at activating a number of mental and cognitive processes, and possibly filling an emotional need.

I hoped that the musical experiences would help the child to discover his innate creativity, express himself through any kind of sound, beautiful, violent, rough or timid; that he would be helped to come out of his loneliness through a world of music.

Juliette Alvin

1978

1   Musical and autistic behaviour

A COMPARATIVE STUDY

Music is a field of multifarious experiences which affect man's mind, body and emotions. It may bring a change in the behaviour of the listener or the player. It penetrates the subconscious and can reveal much of what is hidden there. It can also develop awareness of the environment, whether the individual is so-called normal, or affected by an illness or a handicap. Music in its many aspects is an eminently flexible, adaptable means which can reach an individual at any level of intelligence or education.

This book is a study of the influence of music on the autistic child. It shows how a music therapist can help in creating diverse channels of communication through a number of techniques adapted to his specific difficulties, most of them due to a problem of learning in its widest sense.

Although the book is mainly concerned with long-term cases of autism, I have used material from shorter ones which may add further interest and reinforce certain aspects of the study.

I worked on new approaches to autism, taking into account not only the child's personality but the grave emotional disturbance so frequent in autistic children, and also his level of social adjustment. So far there is no known cure for autism, although there are some treatments which may minimise its effects and improve the child's behaviour and his prospects in life.

The most recent studies on autism seem to show that the child can greatly benefit from a structured therapeutic education. Certain positive pursuits are recognised as beneficial. Already in 1967 Rutter expressed the opinion that:

Nearly all autistic children have specific cognitive defects, normally involving language and perception. Consequently at least at first, methods of instruction involving objects and activities may be more useful than those with emphasis on purely visual stimuli, such as pictures or spoken instructions which are used with normal children but are not suitable to the autistic child.[1]

[1]   Rutter: *Special Education*, vol. LVI, no. 11, p. 19

(It has also been observed that what he sees is not as good as the apprehension of what he touches.) This remark may also apply to what he hears.

These remarks are pertinent to the use of music as a specific means towards the development of the autistic child. The cognitive pathology which affects him seems to produce more than an intellectual blockage. It brings about an inability to relate emotionally and socially, or to become part of the environment – or even to relate one part of his own body to another. The child seems to suffer from a deficiency in grasping a logical process, although he can, to some extent, understand causes and effects in a concrete situation. Music is of value in such a situation since it can be enjoyed at a concrete level without an understanding of abstract processes.

The members of the team around the child – doctors, teachers or therapists – try to make the child use the information he receives from the environment. Since he does not develop in an integrated way, we try to use music as an integrating force, involving in one operation mental, emotional, physical and even social factors, affecting the child directly at his own level of intellectual and emotional tolerance. The techniques should ultimately make sense to the child and enable him to progress at his own pace. Each autistic child is a unique individual whose scattered abilities should come together as much as possible. Perhaps his attraction to music comes from a feeling of being fully involved and more complete within a musical environment.

Each long-term study seems to show three main periods in the child's musical development, clear enough to be related to his development in other fields. In the same way, the child's periods of regression correspond to a regression in his musical progress. In the first phase, music can for a time by-pass the cognitive process and reach the emotional and personality disturbance. The concrete and perceptual aspects of a musical experience can ignore verbal language, and satisfy the child's need for non-verbal self-expression. In the second phase we can observe the child's growing awareness of the increasing human and musical relationship involved in the experience. The third period shows a definite direction towards a specific area in which a particular child can find a satisfying and successful means of self-expression, a source of satisfaction and achievement perhaps for many years to come. The therapy may have given this deprived child the essential support and human understanding he badly needed at the time, as well as a means of self-expression at his own particular level. Music may be for a time a harbour of safety in his difficult passage through life. This often is the case with children under music therapy for a short time. In any case the therapist should assess the child's musical needs and potentials as well as his ability to relate to an adult or to bear demands made on him.

With children possessing some learning ability the three stages of development may proceed more rapidly. The essential is for the child to gain something which can make a deep impression on him and last as long as he can benefit from it. The only dangerous temptation for the parents, the teachers or even the therapist is to hurry the proceedings and try to involve the child in a music-making group when he is not socially or musically ready for it.

The specific musical techniques work mostly on perceptual and cognitive processes. They try to produce psychological results vital to some of the children. The therapeutic application of music has a human purpose, namely to create a human working communication with a child unable to form relationships through the normal channels of love and intelligence. Music therapy often aims at by-passing or removing the emotional or intellectual obstacles standing between him and his environment. It aims at provoking a healthy change of behaviour in his rapport with himself and with those around him.

His relationship with the music therapist has a paramount influence on this change. It rests on the therapist's understanding of his problems and of the application of skills which inspire confidence.

The power of sound

Any sound is what the hearer makes of it, a sensation pleasant or unpleasant. It may evoke pleasant or unpleasant memories or associations through its pitch, tone colour, intensity or duration. We do not always know what provokes the responses to an auditory stimulus of a child who seems to absorb and bottle up so many impressions which he cannot share. His responses to sound or music are often difficult to observe, and even more difficult to interpret. They may be positive or negative, silent or noisy, passive or active. When he is listening you may observe a slight change in his posture, his hands or feet, a sideways look, a sigh or a smile. He may cover his ears or close his eyes, move towards the source of sound or fly away from it, or have a temper tantrum.

Silence is also part of the experience. It is an important factor in music. Silence contains the expectancy of sounds. The temporal organisation of sounds gives shape and meaning to music. It makes demands on cognitive processes when the player, the composer or the listener become conscious of the relationship between sounds organised in a meaningful pattern. This is the way music itself can begin. All techniques described in the following pages are based on using music as a means of communication and creating relationships of different kinds.

RECEPTIVE TECHNIQUES

Receptive techniques include the two auditory processes of hearing and listening. They often work at subconscious level with a penetrating power which the child cannot resist, even if he seems not to perceive it. Hearing is an auditory experience which can work at the low level of a sensation, powerful enough to operate a change or even a breakthrough. The following is an account of various cases in a hospital for autistic children.

Michael, a powerful black boy, autistic, hyperactive, destructive, and possessing uncontrollable physical strength, came to the music room the first day, yelling, kicking and jumping. He had no speech, looked terribly disturbed and at times dangerous. He seemed quite unaware of the environment. After a few days during which I observed his behaviour, I managed to approach him with caution and guarded myself against possible violent reactions, holding his arm with care. Without speaking, I showed him a large cymbal and during a brief moment of quietness I struck the instrument gently and put it near his face. His expression of wonder when he heard the sound turned into a radiant smile, and he looked me in the eyes. The sound had operated an unexpected breakthrough. Under his violent behaviour we found a streak of gentleness, and some musical potential. During the few months he attended the clinic he related to me through the cymbal without difficulty and he never lost his attraction to cymbals of any size. His behaviour improved enough for him to join the dancing group, but he still needed the one-to-one relationship. He also learnt to handle his instruments with care and to listen to the sounds he made on them. His sustained attention was quite remarkable.

Philip was a ten-year old autistic boy who also suffered from severe epileptic fits. In the music room he did not seem to relate to any object or any person. He had not responded to any sound of any kind. One day he was brought to the room as usual, and as usual sat on a chair, crouched on himself, immobile and silent, impervious to any sound or activity around him. He was holding a small wooden stick, a fetish which could not be taken away from him. I tried to attract him for the first time with the song of the nightingale, played on the instrument used by bird watchers. The boy's reaction was immediate. He suddenly came to life, lifting his head and making bird-like movements with his neck. Then he answered the bird by tapping on the table with his stick. It became a real dialogue during which he answered the song with his stick. Later on, he began for the first time to emit loud, shrill sounds. The whole session was recorded and is highly interesting. I used his attraction to the nightingale to channel his response on instruments on which he could use his stick and tap his response, small instruments such as chime bars and tambours. I was full of hope that he would make progress and form some kind of relationship through the music. But he had to leave the clinic to undergo radical treatment and did not come back.

In these two cases, and I could quote many others, the child became aware of the sound he had heard and responded to it actively. Very young autistic children may react in a passive way when they are held on the lap, rocked and hear a song related to the movement of the rocking. This creates almost a prenatal situation, or may fulfil a need in a child who has been unable to experience maternal communication after he was born.

Vibrations can also give the child a sensual pleasure, having a quite distinct effect from the positive one of playing. Patrick, aged seven, was a small-built autistic boy of the hyperactive type. He was obsessive, suspicious and secretive, hiding the instruments under the furniture. His real contact was with the piano. He crouched over the keyboard, played chords with two hands and listened to the vibrations, his eyes half-closed, immobile and almost in rapture. It was a moment of quietness and pleasure in which he was totally involved. The experience created a relationship between his auditory and tactile perceptions, and with the therapist on whose knees he used to sit when at the keyboard.

Music in the child's environment can change his mood and behaviour, from lethargy to activity, or from activity to lethargy. He may be either stimulated or hypnotised by the experience. In the latter case, much harm can be done. The child turns inwards, becomes unaware of his environment, gazes absently, rocks or hums in an obsessive way. Music is to him a way of escape from reality, a means of isolation, a protection against any intruder. The experience results in a deplorable conditioning against which the therapist has to fight, and which must be transformed into a positive situation leading to some perceptual awareness.

I have worked for a long time with a severely autistic girl who had acquired at home the obsessive habit of settling in front of a television or radio set for hours on end. She passed the day humming to herself continuously in a senseless way. The habit had created an unbroken barrier of sounds that made her completely oblivious to anything around her until she was told loudly and sharply 'Stop it'. It made her stop at once. She could then perceive other sounds around her and hear the music she made herself on the autoharp or the chime bars, the sounds of which gave her an obvious pleasure. After a few months when she entered the music room she walked straight to the autoharp and played without humming.

The positive responses of an autistic child to hearing or listening to music are often unpredictable because of his lack of rational behaviour. Receptive techniques can reach the child very deeply, though we do not know exactly how. Nevertheless we can observe signs of pleasure or displeasure, his power of absorption and retention, his wish to renew or avoid the experience.

We can also observe other factors in the child, such as

involuntary physical reflexes produced by the pitch, the volume, the speed or the tone colour present in any kind of sound or music. He may also show signs of fear, withdrawal, exhilaration or indifference. We can also observe the change from hearing to listening and see him entering the field of awareness of sound and music.

The choice of the music to be played to an autistic child is a problem much greater than with a retarded child, whose difficulty is in the discrepancy between his mental and chronological age. A therapist will work at the level at which he can understand and function, and plan a programme accordingly. But with the autistic child such generalisation is not possible on account of the unpredictability of his responses. Many studies have been made all over the world on the way autistic children can listen to music with pleasure or interest, and the kind of music which is successful. Mozart is the name most often quoted, particularly the trumpet or the horn concerto, and some of the quartets or symphonies. But the most diverse and unexpected items are mentioned in individual cases: *My Country* (Smetana), the theme music of the Pallisers, African drums, *Air in D* (Bach), *Dance of the Spirits* on the flute (Gluck), *The Arrival of the Queen of Sheba* (Handel), Stockhausen improvisations, folk dance music, cradle songs by Schubert or Chopin, and so on. It is impossible to quote them all.

Some children seem to prefer music performed live to them by the therapist, and enjoy watching as well as listening. Others prefer the music coming from a machine, perhaps holding the machine on their lap, and controlling the volume, or the stops and starts. Then the child is taking part in the exercise. (These techniques and others are fully described in the case histories.)

In some instances music itself is the primary factor, in others it becomes a secondary factor. But the listening process is a basic part in the building up of a musical relationship between the mysterious world of the child and the reality surrounding him.

Hypnotic conditioned responses must not be confused with the child's spontaneous singing or humming in reaction to a positive sound, heard in a positive active situation. This response is healthy and creative. Many children do sing or hum spontaneously when playing long single sounds on the cello, or strumming long chords on the autoharp, or listening to a favourite recording. Each of them wants to participate actively. When he is ready for something more organised the child can by himself discover a relationship between certain sounds, for example when plucking different strings in turn, or adding another chime bar to his series, or exploring a keyboard, or trying various sounds on a drum. Music is born out of the relationship between sounds, which can work at the most elementary level. At this stage much depends on the sense of freedom and involvement the child experiences in a musical environment, on his receptiveness and his auditory perception.

The environment

The child's ability to function actively may be affected by the physical environment he finds around him. The surroundings play an important part in the sense of musical freedom we wish to give him, freedom to make noises, to shout, to move, to feel safe and not threatened. It should include not only freedom to behave in a certain way and to organise himself, but freedom from fear or obsessions which create emotional, intellectual and social blockages. The two kinds of freedom reinforce one another in a musical experience which at first makes no positive demands on the child. But little by little music can offer him a direction and the structure he so badly needs.

Once the child has acquired a feeling of freedom and becomes more receptive we can offer him the kind of musical order he can benefit from and which depends on his own responses.

The autistic child may recoil from any experience if the environment disturbs him. Some therapists conduct their session in a bare room, which looks very clinical and therapeutic, not always creating the right atmosphere. Even when the environment is made as safe as possible it must be congenial to a child who notices everything around him. This was done at the beginning of the session in the primary school project (p. 67). The arrangement put each of the children in an identical situation and enabled us to make a comparative study of their use of space and their behaviour in a room specially planned for music therapy. There was suitable furniture and a plan allowing for freedom of movement and giving a sense of security.

In my music room Oliver, withdrawn and shy, found a secure place in the arms of a low, comfortable chair in which he settled silently to listen to the cello and let the soft vibrations surround him (pp. 30–31). Another autistic child, Caroline, tense and disturbed, could relax only when she was sitting on a cushion on the floor, listening to a cradle song without words.

In other places and for various reasons music therapy was conducted in very different surroundings. Then I had to adapt my techniques accordingly, to take notice of the size of the room, of its acoustics (which might be too resonant or too dull), of the furniture, of the place of the doors (an important point with the run-away type of child), of the windows through which he can gaze. I had to obliterate the effects of too many disturbing objects, and sometimes to fight against the stimulative brightness of curtains or furniture.

The placing of the furniture and of the various objects to be used has an effect on the behaviour of autistic children. Any change in the arrangement and in the order of things may bring panic, tantrums and withdrawal. Even if withdrawn during the first session an autistic child is likely to keep in his mind a precise, photo-like picture of the situation, to notice any change when he comes again and then be thoroughly upset. Against this obsessive need for sameness which prevents him from learning and adapting, we have to introduce within the expected physical arrangement frequent, small changes that the child should accept without getting upset. But the focal point he expects to see at first when he enters the room should not change. For instance, the main table. But around it we can vary the place where he stands or where he finds the instruments, which can be kept in boxes, on the table or on the floor. These techniques are preventive ones which should not affect the child's sense of security. They begin in the actual surroundings and continue in the musical techniques.

The child may be independent enough to bring some changes himself, and choose various focal points of interest which may be the cymbal (for Oliver) or (for Pamela) the piano, objects with which they seem to identify. Other children create their own territory on the floor or in a corner of the room where they safely gather around them their favourite instruments and play there. Even there some of them feel that the nearby presence of the therapist is an intrusion and move away from her.

Physical contact

Autistic children react differently to the physical proximity of an adult, some of them are reluctant to be touched. This has to be dealt with before any secure relationship can be established between the therapist and the child.

Other children need physical contacts of a motherly kind. Even when autism is believed to be a neurological disorder one cannot ignore the vital importance of mother-child and child-mother relationship from or even before birth. The intimate contact creates the security the baby needs, following the long months of expectancy and growth within the mother's body. The mother of an unresponsive, aloof child and the child himself are likely to experience bitter frustration in their emotional needs. How does the child react if the mother gives up her attempts at communication? He may still have an unexpressed need to be coddled, caressed or rocked even if he does not seem to respond. Such physical need can be answered within a musical experience. The therapist can hold the child on her lap when playing the piano and singing, or rock him gently on her knees. The vibrations surround the child and can reach his subconscious. If the child accepts them, physical contact at any stage can create direct relationship better than words, and may be more meaningful to him. At a more advanced stage than the lullaby, contacts through the hand often provoke a direct communication. For instance, clapping the hands together, face to face, in a 'pat-a-cake' movement is quite revealing. The autistic child usually holds his hands in a bizarre way, stretches his fingers outwards and touches the opposite hand only with his own palm – or he uses his hand as a claw, grabbing the therapist's fingers, and looking up sideways. Full contact is established only when the therapist's and the child's hands tally against one another. It may take time. Direct physical communication can be used when moving together to music, the therapist holding the child's hand. Her fingers, thumb or wrist pressing on the child's hand can speak to him, stimulate or stop him, make him feel secure or under command. They reinforce the effect of the music, and can be firm, caressing, resisting, passive or directing. They should help the child to follow the music or to take the initiative without the use of words.

This special technique can be used when moving to music. The music should be of a non-percussive, melodic type since it is not meant to provoke physical dynamism or involuntary reflexes.

At first the therapist holds the child's hands and helps him to follow the speed of the music which may not be his own. The autistic obsession for a rigid non-stop rocking should be broken down by using a beat slightly faster than that of the child in order to make him conscious of the movement and of the music, since auditory perception in the end should control it.

I used this technique with a severely autistic girl by moving, walking and swinging with her very gently and singing her name on two repeated chords played on a piano at the required speed. She progressed enough to be able to follow the speed of the music and then to participate in a music group instead of rocking away by herself in a corner of the room.

Some non-communicative children who are familiar with the hand contact put their hand forward spontaneously when they see me in the morning.

Little by little the therapist becomes part of the activity. The child associates her with the pleasure and the freedom he experiences. He has come to trust her, even if he still resists or manipulates her, or has a temper tantrum or revolts. The therapist is ready to accept or to forget, never to punish.

ACTIVE TECHNIQUES

All musical activities are primarily directed by auditory perception and rest on the power of sound to penetrate, to be associated with some event and to be remembered. Sounds can be charged with emotions, be memorised at conscious or subconscious level. They may reappear charged with the same emotions as when first perceived. The mental memory of sound and of sequences of sound is vital to the acquisition of verbal or non-verbal language of speech or music, although the two processes function in two different parts of the brain.

Verbal language requires the understanding, coding and decoding of conceptualised symbols. Not so with music, which is considered as a universal means of communication, mostly interpreted as an individual experience in spite of the cultural conditioning attached to it. Nevertheless, the union of speech and melody is widely used in music therapy. We know that music or sound can trigger off a verbal or vocal response which may be the beginning of speech. It indicates a desire to communicate.

The aim is to produce positive contact between the child and his environment, to stimulate him and produce a healthy change in him. We can successfully use very simple, structured activities on a positive perceptual basis. These activities can stimulate some of the cognitive processes necessary to bring together various components of music that the child can relate to one another, for example objects, instruments, sounds, movements, or even words. He can also be offered a choice of activities or techniques in which he can satisfy his preferences. Hearing sounds leads to making sounds, thus we come to active techniques in which the child projects himself in freedom.

The active techniques are aiming at a positive result which it is possible to assess. But we have to take into account that, unlike the retarded child, the autistic child has little motivation towards achievement, no sense of individual standard of progress, although he may find his reward in pleasing an adult.

First stage

At first the child is given freedom to use the instrument or his voice as he likes, provided that he is not destructive. The place where he works is his territory, a safe place where he is investigating and projecting himself, using sounds. Even if he uses unusual techniques, for instance striking a bell upside down, scratching the strings of a guitar or making strange vocal noises, he is creating his own relationship. This non-verbal relationship, an essential one before an inter-personal relationship with the therapist can be formed, may take many forms and go through different stages – the musical instrument usually being at first the intermediary, non-frightening object. The child becomes conscious that the therapist is the provider of a musical, safe and predictable experience. Their initial contact is not necessarily verbal, but built on what music is related to, the room and everything it contains. Much depends on the attitude of the therapist towards the child and music itself.

In the application of active techniques, I work on many perceptual processes.

In the first stage, the child should become aware of sound produced by the voice and the instruments, perhaps beginning with one single sound in which tactile, auditory and motoric processes are combined in one operation. Then we can work on the relation between different sounds, for example the beginning of a musical sequence.

Contact with instruments
Altogether, autistic children can relate to objects better than to persons. In music they can identify with a particular instrument through its tone and its shape. It may become a means of self expression, an intermediary object between them and their environment. The manipulation of this musical object is usually a source of great pleasure to the autistic child. It may even resemble a ritualistic experience. It is beneficial because of the perceptual and motor control processes involved.

The autistic child's attraction to geometrical shapes is well known. We can observe it in his behaviour towards musical instruments. He goes round a tambour with a finger, he touches the strings of a violin or an autoharp not across but following the parallel lines, he builds up constructions of drums, of chime bars arranged in definite shapes. He also makes contact with them through his mouth, sucking or licking the object, smelling it, putting his lips to it. This may be the only real perceptual contact he can make at first with the instrument, before becoming aware of its sound. It gives the child an opportunity 'to feel' by holding the object and examining it. No words or explanations are necessary to give the child the experience of a physical communication. We try to make him relate sound to his own action, including his breathing and the use of his voice as well as his hands and feet.

Rarely have I seen one of my young patients wilfully destroy or damage an instrument even if he treated it violently – if he had chosen it himself. The free choice in which the child is left to express his preference often leads to his identification with the object.

One of them was attracted by three instruments, the cymbal and the autoharp and later on by the cello. At first he used the cymbal to cover his face, before playing it. He tried to pluck the outer strings of the autoharp. Later on he identified with the cello, became quite positive about it, listened to it quietly and enjoyed using the bow on it. In the last year he volunteered to carry it with great care to the music room.

The playing of a musical instrument requires some physical pressure on a surface. This makes the instrument alive to the player, a feeling which may even provoke aggressive behaviour towards it, as did the drum in Kevin's hands (p. 70). The yielding of a plucked string and the visible vibration thus produced gives the child a sense of power. It deeply satisfied Pamela (p. 55) when she chose the longest, most resilient string on the autoharp and kept on repeating the experience.

All instrumental techniques work on the physical resistance of the object itself, which stimulates the perceptual awareness of the child: for instance the resistance of a piano key to pressure, of a string to the plucking or bowing, movement of the drum to the beating of a stick, and so on. We should make the child aware of this resistance, since it can create in him a feeling of mastery and support at the same time.

Instruments such as maracas which are shaken in the air do not give such sense of support to an autistic child. These do not convey the idea of meeting an object in space and in time, connected with a certain pulse or rhythm.

If movement is created by music and expresses it, movement itself creates music, in the vibrations of the vocal chords or a physical action on an instrument. A sound is more obvious to an autistic child when the source of sound and the movement producing it are in his visual field. When he plays on an instrument himself the perceptual and motoric relationship can be greatly developed and lead to better musical results, for instance in the control of speed, strength or magnitude of the movement. It should replace the senseless autistic fiddling with objects and make the child aware of touching an instrument for the purpose of producing a sound. We can observe a similarity between eye or hand avoidance, and the bizarre way some autistic children hold or touch an object. They often seem to be unaware of, or adverse to, the contact necessary to grasp an object, to hold a stick or a beater or a hand cymbal. They may dangle it between the middle fingers and not use their thumb.

We should try to give the autistic child all possible kinds of perceptual contacts based on a feeling of physical resistance. In the autistic child's education much emphasis is laid on manual processes. The remark made above applies equally well to his feet. He often seems unaware of the resistance and support he could experience through the conscious contact of his feet with the ground on which he treads. This is why music and movement closely linked together can create in the child a body image and a feeling of orderly movement starting in the feet.

Music heard on television or radio is mostly based on our diatonic scale, which becomes absorbed unconsciously. Many autistic children seem to be familiar with it even if they cannot sing it. But they can notice when a note is missing and wish to put it right.

I encourage them to pitch their voice on a chime bar within the scale and sometimes add to it words which make sense in the following way:

Ro - bert is a ve - ry good boy.

This produces attention and the retention of an accepted musical form. Much of their auditory training has been on the process.

Wind instruments and voice
The child is made aware of the pressure he puts on an instrument and of the resistance to the pressure. In the playing of wind

instruments the resistance is not in the instrument itself, but in the breathing process, as in voice production. Work with the voice and/or on a wind instrument can develop an awareness of the pressure of the wind entering the lungs and filling them. Both can help one another in giving the child the conscious perception of lips, tongue, jaws and teeth, though the contact with a wind instrument is more positive and concrete.

The developmental process of the production of vocal sounds or of those produced on a wind instrument follow a similar line. They may become more and more refined and controlled. The voice begins at the level of laryngeal noises which can be compared to those produced on a kazoo. Some wind instruments demand finesse of finger movements in different degrees. Some of them are elementary, for instance the melodica, which has fairly large, visible keys and a blowing technique which does not interfere with the intonation of the sound. Some purists may say that the tone is far from beautiful, but it seems to satisfy most autistic children. Other instruments such as the recorder call for much finger skill and accuracy both in the finger tips and the blowing.

Most autistic children can handle a melodica if they have not the attention or the motivation to master a more complex instrument. One has to avoid a feeling of failure which makes the child give up, as happened to Geoffrey with his guitar which he swapped for the autoharp (p. 98).

Musical development

The child becomes increasingly conscious of the different sounds he can play; he uses different notes creating intervals or sequences on chime bars, drums, wind or stringed instruments. The result need not follow a conventional or even predictable pattern, it usually just happens. But the child may wish to repeat the experience and sometimes finds his own way to do it, as did Pamela with the unison (p. 50), which is part of a learning process, namely a search for a pleasant experience based on memory. The child usually does it on his favourite instrument, using any sound he can hear and manipulate. With an autistic child attracted by repetitive processes it is wise to avoid the danger of stereotyped activities. But musical techniques need not be automatic; they are eminently flexible and adaptable. The same melodic pattern can be played on different easy instruments; a simple rhythm such as ♫ ♩ can be tapped on any surface, plucked on a string or blown in a pipe. A scale can be played on chime bars, on the melodica or on the piano. They sound musically the same but in a different way. The child's active or passive response indicates where he has found a communication in the tone colour, the pitch or the volume.

Other children search for weird sounds coming from any object or a musical instrument, or even their own voices. Such positive activities are normal, constructive and often imaginative.

Melody

A melodic pattern begins with the relationship of two or more sounds and leads to some cognitive process. The autistic child seems to possess an innate affinity for certain melodic patterns to which words may be added. Certain intervals may be unpleasant to him, and thus spell danger. He hears music constantly through the mass media and absorbs a number of tunes, incomplete, distorted or sometimes accurate. We can find in him a source of musical tunes or patterns ready to be tapped. Even a number of overseas children may be familiar with nursery rhymes.

One can begin in an elementary way, making the child relate his name to an interval of two notes either sung or played on an instrument familiar to him. I sing his name on a descending major or minor third, or on a fourth which produces no tension. The child may not answer but he is usually listening.

Work on the child's own voice is an essential feature of music therapy with handicapped children. The physiological development of a singing voice is beneficial to a child whose use of sound is so imperfect. It may start when music provokes in him a natural response, namely a desire to make vocal sounds, sometimes singing or humming to himself. The work should begin with a vocal, not a verbal process, first listening to any sound the child can utter and answering him in the same manner. This was done with Geoffrey through a technique of vocal regression, which helped him to become aware of his own voice at the pre-verbal level. The process was dissociated from the use of words which often produces a rigid automatism and should be avoided. (p. 77).

The voice of an autistic child is often strange, inflexible and rigid. It can greatly be improved by helping him to breathe better, to hold a long sound, to pitch and modulate his voice on a vowel such as AH or UH.

The child can be made aware of a vocal process through the drawing of a line showing the movement of the sound when he is actually singing. This line drawn under his eyes is the metric representation of the sound he emits, when he watches the movement of the pen on the paper, its length corresponding to the duration of the note he is singing, from its beginning to its end.

The same technique applies to the modulation of the child's voice when he sings an interval played on two chime bars in his visual field:

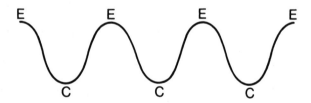

This technique can become increasingly complex: the child can follow the line with his finger – or draw the line himself when he is actually singing – or play the chime bars at the same time, and so on. The process can be applied to the playing of a wind instrument such as the melodica where the duration of a sound is related to the breathing process. The drawing may be the first step towards the understanding of musical symbols.

The living contact with a sound the child has produced himself vocally or on an instrument, and of which he becomes increasingly aware, still makes little demand on a cognitive process. The result of the action is immediately apprehended by the child. Nevertheless one can observe the emergence of a certain mental activity. The child is beginning to grasp the concept of causes and effects at a very simple level. He may be able to learn how to produce certain sounds when wanted and make them meaningful. Or to prepare a movement leading to a predictable result. For instance he can apply the fist or hand technique alternately to play 'soft' or 'loud' on a tambour; he can stretch his arm before playing a loud note on the cymbal; or direct the movement of the bow on a given string. Many of these techniques are described in the case histories. They help the child to become conscious of his own mastery over sound and movement.

Rhythm

On the whole, rhythm seems to work better than melody on a primary level. It can be absorbed physically and cannot be taught. It works on physiological responses but only rarely produces a vocal or verbal reaction in an autistic child as melodic patterns do. Only a few autistic children seem to possess an innate sense of rhythm in movement. They are not aware of their obsessive movements following a monotonous beat, which in itself is not a rhythm.

The perception of sound associated with a specific movement can help the child to develop some rhythmical sense, especially when the experience is concrete and works on combined perception.

Rhythm consists of patterns of sounds of different duration and accentuation. I have found that the easiest one to absorb, remember and use is the following one: crotchet, crotchet, minim. It can be the basic common denominator integrating a music making or a dancing group.

The metric representation of this rhythmical pattern can make a direct and deep impression on the mind of an autistic child, as most children can associate it with corresponding verbal rhythms: for example, 'apple pie' or 'go to sleep'.

With more advanced children I have attempted to make the rhythmical pattern more complex. Some of the children were able to grasp the meaning of the following symbols and to relate them to sounds and movements:

Those were transferred later on to proper musical notation. It enabled some groups of autistic children to master their individual drumming part and even to follow the score (p. 107).

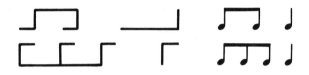

Many other techniques can be used, taken first as the most elementary stage where cognitive processes are not essential, and then increased gradually to a further stage. For instance, activities related to numbers.

I may begin with a couple of chime bars on the table or on the floor, gradually increasing their number, or sometimes introducing a black one among them. To some of the children, a series of, say, eight notes represented a global number, to others a series of units.

Rhythm includes the use of silence. The ability to begin or to stop playing implies a mastery of movement in time and space without which rhythm cannot exist. It demands a mental effort especially when it is not part of a stereotyped pattern. The ability to stop allows another sound played by another person to be heard. It is part of a socialising process which can work first on a one-to-one basis, and then be applied to group work. This gradual development enables the children to dance together, or at a higher level, to become part of a music group.

In these activities which have a concrete basis, I become more and more of a working partner to the child, who is increasingly ready to accept the demands I or the music make on him. He has reached a higher stage in the learning process. He has also learnt to form with me a stable relationship through which we share the music.

Second stage

So far the work and the techniques described may not have been specific demands on the child's cognitive processes, and they could not have taken him very much further. They aim at giving him perceptual and motoric awareness; the ability to produce sounds in complete freedom within a safe environment. He acquires a rudimentary, unfettered means of self-expression in an area of discovery and experiment, doing spontaneous things in his own way. Gradually the child learns to accept my participation after becoming conscious of my presence in the room. I increase our physical non-verbal contacts, for instance in sharing the instrument at close proximity. I get involved myself, as a musician, in helping his musical efforts. For instance, I may add an integrating part or an ostinato basso to his scattered or disorderly improvisations. In this way I add another dimension to his music. I offer him the musical, non-verbal co-operation which is more supportive than words. The child knows instinctively that he and I can build together an orderly and satisfactory musical form. Even when one can go no further, music, particularly the use of the voice and instruments, can give immense satisfaction to the child, and he himself gives in return as much as he can.

The children's performances from the most elementary stage are mostly improvised, free from any established rules. I have recorded many of them. They show usually the development of a musical personality, an assertion of self and some progress in vocal and instrumental techniques.

Improvisation

I have taken hours of recordings of the sessions with autistic children under my care. It is possible to extract from them examples of the children's spontaneous improvisations. These extracts show the musical personality of each of the children.

The improvisations certainly reveal subconscious processes at work – there are some happenings by chance, others are deliberate, perhaps when the child has discovered a sound he likes, or a pleasant sequence which he tries to reproduce. His response to hearing another sound in the room varies according to his state, and has social and perceptual implications. One can detect the development of the mastery of a better, more orderly technique, even if the improvisation is not orderly. But however poor or rich is the musical result, the personality of the child comes through. The obsessive type plays in an obsessive way. The imaginative, independent child uses space, different instruments and changes his speed or his dynamics.

The remark one can make about all these children is that their musical spontaneity and even inventiveness is baffling when one tries to use it in order to teach something more orderly or logical. The development which has taken place in the spontaneous approach is rarely usable in learning the normal way.

How conscious is the search for or the repetition of certain patterns? Even if they are part of a longer improvisation they can not be used as a basis for a musical development. I have sometimes tried to insert them into a larger musical structure, but the child does not seem to recognise them or to find anything familiar in them, even repeated verbatim.

One can easily observe that the child who improvises freely is in a state of semi-consciousness, although this creative state may disappear when conscious processes take over. Then his cognitive deficiency may make him turn to rote learning and imitation of something from outside, not from within himself.

Through improvisation his instrumental technique usually improves. Very often the improvisations sound like an undirected and a mysterious search. Sometimes they seem to express a definite mood of anger, revolt or withdrawal. Quite often, we find at first a certain amount of rumination until something more like 'our music' appears. Even if shortlived, it has a brief temporal form.

The mastery over and use of instruments can incite the child to commit himself to improvise for a longer time because he can experiment in a larger field. For instance, we can observe the effect of glissandos on a glockenspiel, which provokes activity and attention as well as a marked speeding-up in the tempo.

It is obvious that very few of these improvisations can be judged or appreciated against normal musical standards. Their interest lies elsewhere, perhaps in their close link with the world of autism. Nevertheless, we cannot rule out the fact that a few autistic children possess a special gift for music, combined with exceptional physical and imitative ability. However, none of the children described in this book possessed this special gift.

FURTHER DEVELOPMENT

After the first building-up period, which can last for many months, one should come to a stage where it is possible to integrate in a musical situation everything the child can offer – in other words to enlarge the field of action, to work on the relationship of sound with numbers, words, movement, reading and so on.

During this second stage the child should develop a sense of musical, social behaviour towards his instruments and the use of his voice, towards himself, his need for self-expression, his relationship with me, and the demands made by music itself on his attention and good will.

All the techniques rest on pleasure – the pleasure of sound itself, of handling an instrument, the pleasure of repeating a satisfactory pattern or sound, the pleasure of asserting oneself in a secure environment. The child sometimes becomes conscious of what musical behaviour implies, and of the demands it makes on him. He has to face and to control himself during the musical activities.

Even if his musical achievement is minimal, but provided he is mature enough to do so, then he can join a music-making group. There he can learn social behaviour, how to tolerate others, and to be accepted. This can be the first step towards social maturation. But intellectual maturation can grow only through the workings of cognitive processes.

In order to proceed further than the stage at which we have now arrived, it is necessary to involve a process of learning which we cannot ignore any more. This is not only educational, but related to the child's whole maturation. It is the growth of self-knowledge and his awareness of his own place in the environment. He should now try to control his behaviour and get a sense of real identity. The child's musical maturation depends on the way he can be aware of the content of the music, and how he can follow it. When he listens to music, he should be helped to recognise certain patterns he is familiar with: for instance a scale, a series of five notes, the tone colour of various instruments, or a rhythmical pattern. In the same way he should become aware of the continuity of movement necessary to play a part on an instrument or to sing. He then becomes conscious of, and has to adapt to, the temporal aspect of music as a global experience. The apprehension of music involves mental operations, such as the expectation and memory of sound, the awareness of melodic intervals and rhythmical patterns as well as the apprehension of intensity, frequency, speed or tone colour. The temporal and repetitive elements in music are appealing to a child who often fills his time with repetitive patterns of behaviour. Repetitive elements in music can help him to relate to it, but they have to be part of a larger structure in order not to become obsessive or stereotyped.

When the child plays, the process makes some mental demands on his ability to relate thought and action, and leads to a predictable result. The experience involves the memory of a sound related to a prepared movement and to its result in tone colour, intensity or duration. Musical understanding cannot go very far without fairly complex mental operations usually beyond the intellectual power of an autistic child. Even if he is able to follow, remember and repeat a tune (a temporal process), he may find it impossible to grasp several simultaneous sounds. His reaction to harmony or chords may, stay at the non-intellectual stage of a sensuous impression, based on the tone colour of superposed sounds.

His understanding of music as structured sound may remain at the level of his understanding of the organisation of spoken language, namely as a structure which develops from isolated words, nouns, verbs, qualificatives and so on, which the child can grasp in isolation. The use of certain single words of action associated with musical activities can provoke a specific mental response leading to a predictable result – some words bear an emotional connotation and help the child to express himself; others reinforce the sense of purpose of a certain movement.

Opposites based on extremes such as 'soft, loud', 'fast, slow', 'big, small' and so on are usually effective because they provoke action. Other words indicate a movement: blow; tap; hit; clap. Or a movement in space: right, left, middle, end, up, down; or a physical action: run, jump, hop, walk, stop. The use of simple words associated with musical activities creates a relationship and makes some demands on the child's memory, on his motor control.

The development of speech is crucial to an autistic child. It depends on auditory perception first, hence the importance of music related to words. Most autistic children are searching for sound in their environment, a search which often reveals itself through scratching a surface or tapping on it. We should direct their search towards meaningful sounds produced on various objects with various techniques. Thus the instrument may become a field of conscious exploration. Sounds can be imitative and associated to another experience in the child's memory such as the two notes of the cuckoo song or of the ambulance signal. We can also use the ticking of a clock, the bell of the alarm, the burr of an engine, the squeaking of a wheel. We follow a modern trend of the use of any sound in music. Then we seem to return to a magic conception of sound expressing life and giving life to an object – a conception which may easily be part of the world of the autistic child.

I have tried to open to him the never-ending musical circle which gradually encompasses sound, music, objects, movement, voice and words and in which they are integrated.

One-to-one-relationship

Most autistic children are on the defensive, hidden behind a barrier of silence, immobility, hyperactivity, tantrums or avoidance. They also are manipulative and frequently escape into their own world of obsessions, rituals, loneliness and incongruity.

Their behaviour seems to be the result of anxiety and fear of a bewildering world with which they cannot communicate, to which they cannot relate or belong.

In the world of music the autistic child can feel safe, and sometimes act normally like an ordinary child. I treat him accordingly. I offer him to share musical experiences at his level, on equal terms with him. Week after week, month after month, year after year I aim at becoming to him a truly predictable person, firm enough to give him the support and the stability he badly needs and totally undisturbed by his outbursts or his withdrawals. In short, I accept him without reservation. I try to give him kindness and understanding, without showing the compassion or even the love to which he may not respond. I wish to gain his trust in a world which bewilders him.

Moreover, he is in need of a means of self-expression and self knowledge, but not necessarily through a sense of achievement or praise. To expect too much or too little from an autistic child is equally dangerous. I often have to approach him physically, intellectually or emotionally in a tentative, cautious way since a step backward with such a child may be irreversible.

I have to deal with his manipulative behaviour. This is proof of how sensitive and perceptive he is of the people around him, in the same way as he perceives all the details in a room without looking at them. This acute perception does not seem to be related to an emotional sensitivity. It is rather a defensive mechanism. The child knows perfectly when I will allow myself to be manipulated, and when not.

On these general premises I have been able to build up a satisfactory relationship with the autistic children under my care. After some time I have been able to make on them demands which would have seemed to be impossible at the beginning. Their confidence in me as a musician is real and has given me an authority. Furthermore, I do not recall an instance where I have become a mother figure. It is the musical instrument which has borne any transference.

Sometimes I have deliberately stayed out of the musical activities in order to give this insecure child a sense of independence and initiative in a safe environment, and the means to express himself spontaneously through music. He may then show a need for love which I am ready to answer, a need which came out with those who have built a lasting friendship with me.

Group relationship
The social integration of a handicapped child is the ultimate aim of a therapeutic treatment. Autistic behaviour is in essence anti-social

and reveals a state in which the child's power of communication is gravely impaired.

An adult is often able to create with the autistic child an interpersonal relationship which may play an important part in the child's life. But socialisation implies more than a one-to-one relationship. It must spread out to various members of the community.

Musical activities can follow a general pattern of social development, according to the child's maturity and ability to communicate rather than to his musical achievement. He may begin on his own, sing or play an instrument, or in a duet, sing with his mother or play with his teacher. Then I can try to make him join a larger group like a trio, a band, or an orchestra. Such steps can follow the gradual musical development of an autistic child and help him to integrate socially, provided that he can respond to a musical common denominator such as speed or a rhythmical pattern which unites the members of the group.

The ambition of a special school is often to have a music group functioning in an acceptable way. With autistic children this represents a difficult task, but it can sometimes be tried.

I worked for several years in an autistic unit with ten children. They ranged from three to fifteen years in age, belonged to different races and backgrounds. The only thing they had in common was autism, the greatest obstacle to socialisation.

I had prepared them individually for many months towards the pleasure of enjoying together a familiar experience, moving and dancing to music at a certain speed, using a rhythm they had absorbed.

We used a series of 20 different folk dances played on records or on the piano. They were stimulating but not percussive, at the right speed, with a ♫ ♩ pattern in the bass and a clear flowing melody in the treble. The three assistants, the children and myself used all the space available in the room. The dancing group consisted of a wide circle, each child holding hands and stretching his arms as widely as possible following the speed of the music. All the children learnt to stop and keep silent when the music stopped, and start again when the music began again. They also learnt to stop moving to let a child perform individually in the middle of the group. They followed the movement corresponding to the words that they had mastered individually, such as 'lift your knees' – 'touch your toes' – 'clap your hands', and so on.

We tried to make each child accept some kind of interpersonal relationship, two children holding hands and whirling together, or meeting face to face with an assistant or another child. If a child resisted or flopped down on the floor, he was put in the middle of the moving circle.

At first some children opted out, escaped, hid themselves or had a temper tantrum. But a shared physical activity seemed to break down defences and be acceptable to them. We encountered in the group all the emotional, psychological and social situations connected with shared activities. Some children who became possessive towards an adult, manipulated and disrupted the group. Others became obsessed by the presence of another child they wanted to dominate, to attack or to push away. The physical contact with each child was through holding hands and everything it entails, from children who resist being touched to those who hang on to you desperately and cannot let go. In the middle of a real enjoyment many deep feelings such as resistance, obsession, jealousy, possessiveness, aggressiveness and others come out. Music and movement seemed to create an environment in which these feelings could be acknowledged and dealt with.

A group working together, whether formed of normal or disturbed children, presents the well-known problems of acceptance and tolerance. Ultimately, the pleasure our autistic boys and girls experienced in moving together to music helped them to relate to one another. It became a socialising experience between children who had very little in common except their handicap.

The success of the activity was very much due to the dynamism of the assistants (at the ratio of at least one to two children) taking part. Anyone dealing with disturbed children can understand that the adults taking part in the group were put to a severe test of physical stamina and psychological endurance. To move, sing and speak, to stimulate some children and relax others, to direct movements and keep on moving cheerfully needs patience and a deep sense of purpose.

2 Case histories

OLIVER[1]

Oliver was sent to me for music therapy by a consultant psychiatrist when he was just over eight years old. He had been twice diagnosed at the age of five and later at the age of seven as autistic and mute autistic. He suffered from noise phobia. He had been born with a cleft palate and operated on at an early age. Later on, as he seemed to be deaf, he was tested with a hearing aid. It is possible that his phobia was the result of this distressing experience. When he came to me he could not tolerate any noise, not even the sound of his own voice. He expressed himself with inaudible sounds or gestures. Even the anticipation of a loud noise would upset him and he covered his ears in panicky defence. His mother had observed in him at an early age a number of disturbing features, such as keeping awake the whole night, rocking, breaking windows, keeping his head down continuously, not looking, jumping from great heights without fear, moving objects aimlessly, running his hands over rough surfaces until they bled.

The boy had gone through various periods of development and regression during which his autistic behaviour had become more pronounced, characterised by ritualistic gestures, obsessions, unwarranted anxiety, periods of tension, withdrawal or blankness. He scarcely spoke, since although he had acquired a small vocabulary and could understand simple language he could not converse. He experienced no satisfaction from any manual activity, and showed no sense of achievement.

The family life had been somewhat unsettled. The mother lived in a world of fantasy, the father after having been unemployed

---

[1]   J. Alvin: *Study in Depth of an Autistic Child*, 1971, British Society for Music Therapy
J. Alvin: 'Work with an Autistic Child', *British Journal of Music Therapy*, vol. I, no. 3, 1971

for a long time was now trying to run a small business. There were two healthy siblings, Oliver being the third child.

Oliver attended a day hospital for treatment. As he seemed to respond to music, the child psychiatrist thought that music therapy could help with the treatment of Oliver's problems of communication and ego development. Oliver's progress in music therapy was related to his development in other fields, such as speech or reading, and was discussed regularly with the members of the therapy team.

Oliver was a challenging case of silent withdrawal. When a child resists, yells or expresses anger one can find a field of action and reaction. But with Oliver, locked up in his silent world, there was little one could hold on to. He was apathetic, passive and almost mute. He kept his head down, his eyes averted and downcast. He seemed to be always physically and mentally exhausted. He was docile and spineless. Physically he was a beautiful child, very refined, with well-shaped hands. He was small for his age, and walked in a strange manner. All his movements were inhibited. But under his apathy he sometimes suffered from violent attacks of nervous tension. His jaws then became set and rigid, and sometimes he cried without apparent reason. He could not keep attentive for more than one or two minutes. Then he refused to go on, whispering to himself 'no more'.

First period

At first there was no communication, he did not look at me and seemed to be unaware of the environment. During the first session I assessed Oliver's negative or positive reactions to various musical experiences. I made him see and hear a number of musical instruments: chime bars, piano, drums, cymbals, flutes, maraccas, cello. He showed no reaction to rhythm, and drums did not attract him. He showed no inclination towards any instrument. He refused to open his mouth to sing. But he reacted positively to beautiful sustained, resonant sounds, especially on the cello. When he heard them he looked up and followed the sounds attentively, until they had died out. The vibrations seemed to create for him a protective environment which made no demands on him.

I planned for him a long-term programme related in some way to the psychotherapy and the speech therapy he was already being given at the hospital. My approach was based on a number of psychological processes and techniques adapted to the boy's innate reactions to music and to his behaviour. I hoped that, in time, music could reach his subconscious and bring out his feelings of aggression, fear or anger; that it could relieve his anxieties and tensions, provide a non-threatening environment in which he could express himself freely and find his identity; help him to develop his perceptual awareness and motor control.

I hoped that the music sessions would help him to create with an adult the one-to-one relationship of trust and security he badly needed. I also hoped to bring some creative beauty in the life of a badly deprived child.

From the beginning I used receptive and active techniques to establish communication. Oliver's response to resonant sounds was already a form of communication which had to be transformed into a pleasurable and purposeful experience during which he would hear and create music himself.

For several months he started the session by sitting in an arm chair looking quite lost and vulnerable. I did not use words but played to him on my cello, facing him. I chose extremely soft music usually in the middle register, either tunes familiar to him or improvisations. Little by little I increased the repertoire and the length of each piece from ten to 60 seconds. He listened well, closing his eyes. When he had enough he just whispered 'no more'. He never showed any motivation to touch the cello, his pleasure was in listening to it, although the motivation came later.

Instruments and the voice are the musical intermediaries which create communication. The instruments I offered Oliver and which became his 'orchestra' were those which did not require any special technical skills and gave immediate satisfaction. They provided an easy but basic means of training in perceptual awareness, auditory discrimination and in motor control. The instruments included eight chime bars, a glockenspiel, maraccas, various drums, flutes, hand cymbals, one large orchestral cymbal and a wooden board. We also used a piano and a cello, and cassettes with a small tape recorder which served various purposes.

The pieces we used for listening had to be extremely short, expressing a definite mood, and possibly provoking non-verbal imagery in the boy's mind. I hoped that at a later stage we could experiment with the boy's reactions to unusual kinds of musical sounds.

The geometrical shape of certain musical instruments can be particularly significant to an autistic child – Oliver related to circular objects such as a cymbal or a drum, to the parallel lines seen on a keyboard, a glockenspiel or a series of chime bars. He seemed either to avoid contact with certain objects, or to use them in an incongruous manner. For instance, he often avoided using his thumb to handle a stick and for a long time held the beater dangling between his middle fingers. When sitting at the piano he refused for several months to open his hands on the keyboard. He went gradually from striking the keys with his folded arms, to using his clenched fist or the palm of his hand, fingers turned upwards. Little by little, as his tactile perception developed, he learnt how to place his hands and fingers normally on the keys. He possessed beautiful hands, with long tapered fingers, which many pianists would have envied.

His attraction to geometrical shapes, crosses, triangles, angles or lines showed in the way he tried to arrange his small instruments or his beaters and sticks. I let him use them as he had arranged them himself. Parallel lines seemed to give him a sense of security, and it took a long time for him to accept a break in the normal continuity of a row of keys, or strings or bars. Most autistic children cannot bear changes in their environment, including changes of sound-producing objects. These were normally arranged in a certain order. Oliver was very conscious of their arrangement which, if disturbed, could create in him a state of fear or bewilderment. Therefore, on the piano, he had to strike each key in turn from left to right. He counted them silently and uttered a number when he reached the last top note, a reaction one can observe in many autistic children. The speed at which Oliver struck each key was even and orderly, about 152 per minute. I had to find techniques which would not create fear or panic in Oliver but which at the same time would be flexible enough to be adaptable to his speed or beat.

Oliver was extremely conscious of time as a rigid, protective element. He could identify with any object which measures time, ticks and revolves, such as clocks or watches or a metronome. They gave him a sense of support. But at the same time, he adopted in his music an unrelenting automatic beat impervious to any change – from within or without. There seemed to be in Oliver a pendulum regulating his rocking, a rigid musical beat of about 108 per minute. We know that changes spell danger to an autistic child and can create a state of panic. Oliver learnt how to alter the speed of the metronome safely by moving the weight up and down the metal column. He learnt how to follow its movement first with his hand from left to right, then on the two chime bars placed in front of the metronome. This activity created no distress in Oliver. He identified with the machine. When he was lethargic, the joke was to use a large key 'to wind him up' and he functioned better afterwards. The willingness or ability of an autistic child to alter his own speed in music indicates a definite split in his defences, and may even amount to a musical breakthrough. It took three years to achieve this with Oliver. The day he improvised on his orchestra a series of accelerandos and ritardandos without being prompted was a significant step towards his liberation. It was also a proof of his growing musical identity.

The cymbal
It took some time for Oliver to become skilful at manipulating musical instruments. He was particularly attracted by the large orchestral cymbal on a stand. He identified with it rapidly, walking round it, crouching under it and touching it. He seemed to be lost in its long vibrations. I used this identification to fight his worst phobia. He became ready to accept the sounds he himself made on it even when they were pretty loud. After a while he learnt how to control their volume and to prepare himself for their impact. On several occasions he let himself go, hitting the instrument furiously and covering his ears at the same time. These were some of the rare violent emotional outbursts he experienced in the music room. Otherwise it was

obvious that the musical vibrations which surrounded him acted as a kind of protection and helped him to communicate safely with the world around him.

There is, hanging on the wall of the music room, a beautiful golden sun clock. He used to play to it, standing, looking up and beating on a chime bar. In spite of the ritualistic, arresting character of the performance, it took a positive meaning when the boy struck on his chime bar the hour he could read on the dial.

At first my relationship with Oliver was unobtrusive. It consisted mainly in giving him musical support and in guiding his efforts. He needed stimulation and help to keep attentive long enough and remember. Our relationship developed slowly and safely in a peaceful way. Oliver's pleasure in music became gradually deeper – he loved coming to the music room and was always upset if he had to miss it. I think that the satisfaction the boy experienced during his music therapy sessions did not come from a sense of achievement, or the desire to please me. He seemed to be in need of music, and of the spontaneous happiness he found in musical experience. No doubt he felt I could help him to find it. After a few months he always expressed the desire that I should play and support him during his improvisations, or sit with him at the keyboard. He often leant on me affectionately when we sat next to one another. Our relationship of trust and understanding grew steadily. It had begun when I played to him on my cello, while he, a frail, vulnerable child, afraid of words, sunk in a big armchair, listened for a brief moment to music.

The music which penetrated without imposing itself was the intermediary non-verbal message between him and me, and has created a continuous rapport between us. The message very often came from Bach, Schubert or de Falla among many others.

Just before he was nine years old, Oliver suffered from a period of severe regression probably due to family trouble. With an autistic child, such regression is always possible. In consequence the music therapy sessions suffered as Oliver's behaviour became more incongruous and purposeless. He went round the room inspecting everything around him in an aimless manner. But after a few weeks, we could continue as before, not having lost any of the musical progress.

Second period

Music can help a disturbed child to develop from chaos to order and give him a means of self-expression according to his needs and his ability. In order to achieve this, the spontaneous freedom of the child must become more structured and give him a supporting frame, together with the feeling that he is progressing. The initial source of such development is the music which exists in him, as in every child, ready to be aroused and to express his personality.

Oliver by nature was a musical colourist, sensitive to tone colour, discriminating, eclectic and imaginative. Resonance seemed to be the main auditory pleasure he found in music. His perceptual development was motivated by his search for tone colour and acoustical vibrations. He learnt how to produce different kinds of sounds on the same instrument, for instance tapping with his finger tips or his fist on a drum, or using a beater; making glissandos or separate notes on the xylophone, playing loud or soft on the chime bars. At first his movements were erratic and uncontrolled, but his ear guided him to find the auditory pleasure he needed. This was never allowed to become an obsession. But his performance was spoilt by a rigid, obsessive sense of speed, a refusal to alter his beat once he had found it. When he had become familiar with a number of instruments, I placed him in the centre of the safe territory of his orchestra, free to use it as he liked. At first his improvisations were chaotic, without control of time, space or form. He played all over the instruments in the same way as he behaved with objects in the room, touching them aimlessly without seeming to look at them. But after a few weeks, in the middle of the chaos, one could detect his preference for, or his avoidance of, certain instruments. Gradually, his performance improved as his manipulation of instruments became more conscious and skilful. Oliver could express his musical personality through his free choice of instruments. His refusals too were significant.

Many non-speaking children find a substitute or a compensation in the use of a wind instrument. But with Oliver it failed. I found that anything related to his mouth distressed him, including visits to the dentist. This is the reason why he did not want a flute or pipe among his instruments.

His behaviour with his instruments, two of them in particular, became increasingly marked. He went from identifying with them cautiously to using them as a means of self-projection.

In spite of his noise phobia, Oliver after a few months could tolerate the loud sounds he made himself on the large orchestral cymbal. He let out passionate feelings unsuspected in such a quiet child, playing very loud and fast, usually covering his ears but going on. Sometimes he stopped and said to himself 'no more'. At other times, he beat very gently, leaning over the instrument and listening a long time to the vibrations fading away. Sometimes he settled under the instrument and listened to it from below. His new tolerance of the noise he produced himself helped him not to be afraid of the sound of his own voice.

From his first visit to the music room Oliver had shown an obsession with wooden surfaces, touching or tapping on them aimlessly. During the second year I offered him a large mahogany board on which he could satisfy his obsession in a purposeful way, since it could be used among the instruments of his orchestra. He was much attracted by it and began by testing all the kinds of sounds he could produce on it, on top or bottom or at the back. He liked best the sounds he made near the edges. He adopted this board as a percussion instrument. After this he seemed not to be attracted any more by the other wooden objects in the music room.

Improvisation

Oliver's orchestral free improvisations were at the centre of his music therapy. They also included my musical participation, if needed, as a partner, never as an authority. The growth of his identity was continuously reflected in the musical development of his improvisations.

The chronological recordings of his improvisations show the emergence of some organisation through imitation and repetition, a process based on the pleasure of hearing particular sounds at his disposal. Although none of his first improvisations is longer than one minute, an analysis of them reveals a growing personality.

The appearance of a rhythmical pattern in his improvisations is striking. One can hear in the middle of a series of notes of a similar value, two rapid repeated notes which may be taken for a rhythm. But quite often there seems to be a physical compulsion to repeat the same sound one or more times, and it is not an organisation of time values.

Improvisation on different instruments

(♩ = 100 p. m.)

'no more'

Gradually Oliver began to use certain musical patterns he had become conscious of, the ragtime, or an interval of a sixth or a third. He could memorise these on his series of chime bars. With time, his improvisations became longer, but they usually petered out or stopped abruptly. During the second period the process became more elaborate and his use of his instruments more discriminating. For instance, he used the cymbal to make an opening statement and became more assertive. Later on, his style became more and more flexible. He could play at a slower speed and express relaxation, space and harmony. He then became able to change his speed during the improvisation. Some of his musical efforts seemed to be built around an accelerando in the middle and a ritardando at the end. But they hardly ever increased in length.

During his improvisations I gave him from the piano the support he needed and often asked for, by playing an ostinato at his own chosen speed on an octave at the bass. The rest I left to his initiative, unless I felt that he needed some stimulant in hearing high-pitched notes, or a staccato rhythm pattern. He rarely imitated what he heard, and so in one sense his work could be described as truly creative.

Duet with J. A.

Oliver; chime bars and glockenspiel
J.A. : piano

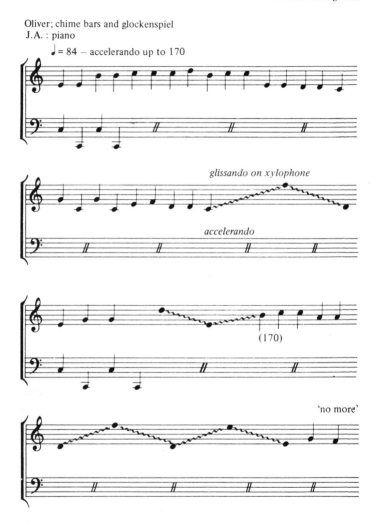

At a later date Oliver came in close contact with the piano and lost his obsession for an unbroken series of sounds played up and down with one finger. At first the result of his hands striking the keys was chaotic, very unrhythmical and lacking the harmonious resonances he produced on his orchestra. But the use of the keyboard produced other results: an awareness and control of individual fingers, independence of the two hands, the use of a considerable territory of keys at his disposal. It made him lose his inhibitions within the framework of an easy physical activity. He began to sing spontaneously when at the keyboard in spite of the disorder of the musical result. It was the beginning of what I was hoping to achieve later.

Voice

His singing of syllables on the five-note sequence showed a marked development in his voice. His voice was typical, without rhythm, and he could not modulate it. When he came to me, his speech was a series of confused noises which seemed to make sense to him but had to be interpreted. It was difficult to know how much he realised his verbal deficiency since he was then not able to keep attentive long enough to perceive and remember sounds. There, music could help him to develop some auditory awareness, especially with regard to his own voice.

I tried to make him listen more attentively by bringing a resonant chime bar close to his ear, with the aim of provoking some kind of vocal response. At first he emitted just a whisper, imitating or answering the sound. After long and patient trials, he could hold a sound long enough to modulate his voice, usually on what approximated to a descending minor third. At that stage I introduced him to the autoharp. The physical movement necessary to pluck a full chord on the instrument helped him to breathe better and prevented the tightening of the larynx.

The second stage was more elaborate. I asked him to stand up and tried to make him conscious of breathing processes, to prompt him to open his mouth and hold a sound. I sustained his efforts with full chords on the piano. Later on he could imitate some rhythmical patterns on vocal sounds, for instance those he was learning in speech therapy, such as 'bababa' or 'mama'.

The next step consisted in making him use voice and instruments combined and to synchronise what he could already master. For instance, in the tune of 'Hickery-Dickery Dock', we used a vertical glockenspiel on which the mouse went up, followed by the striking of one on the orchestral cymbal, with the run down of the mouse represented by a glissando down the glockenspiel. This was one of the activities based on the co-ordination of one-syllable words in a sentence with a meaningful movement. At first, Oliver needed much help and much prompting. In the end he was successful, as recordings made at the time show. On these occasions he did not mind listening to the play-back of his own voice mixed with the sounds of the instruments although he had objected to the recordings of his voice alone.

Listening to music

The receptive or listening techniques I used with Oliver were of two kinds: either to live music which I played on the cello or the piano, or recorded music on a cassette player. During the first period he was so withdrawn, almost inaccessible, that I played to him in an intimate way on the cello, sometimes with the mute on.

The music he seemed to like best was of a gentle kind with a continuous flowing rhythm such as the Schubert Cradle song, *Kumbaya*, or a minuet by Bach – not longer than one and a half minutes. Strong accents or dissonances seemed to disturb him. Later on when I felt that he could respond to more colourful experiences, I used various types of orchestral music on a cassette. He seemed to respond more to specific elements of sound, pitch, volume, tone colour or duration than to a piece as a whole. This helped me to choose music able to reach him.

He listened well to short extracts from *Vltava* by Smetana, or Spanish music, country dances, Chinese or Indian music. Among these he did not seem to have a strong preference for any particular kind of music until something unexpected happened. He became fascinated by some atonal music by Stockhausen, containing series of long parallel sounds within a non-accentuated structure. He crouched over the tape recorder, listening to it for more than twelve minutes. The music obviously reached him deeply. In a remote way it sounded a little like his own improvisations.

Autistic children relate easily to machines. They are often good at controlling them and do not seem to be afraid of them. A cassette recorder gives the child an opportunity to use this unexpected manipulative skill and to direct it towards a pleasurable and organised purpose. A small cassette player placed on his lap increases the feeling of relationship. He can direct the experience, stop, start, increase or decrease the volume, but cannot change the speed of the music. Oliver learnt how to record his own performance and how to play it back. The mastery gave him a deep sense of satisfaction. I entrusted him with the machine and the operation of it, which gave me a good idea of his span of attention, his actual tolerance of intensity, and which piece he preferred. It was one of his rare moments of independence, and helped towards the growth of his identity.

We often recorded his own improvisations, as a reward for his having done his best. But it took several months for him to recognise his own performance in the play-back, since this depended on his auditory recall. But in spite of the praise I gave him, it did not give him any sense of standard or achievement. He was pleased when I looked pleased. His conscious musical enjoyment increased, together with his auditory development, when he became more aware of form and meaning in music. He could then listen to longer pieces, follow a musical development and anticipate the end.

It was at that time that his improvisations came to a.full blossoming. He was still a child but he was nearing adolescence, and his autism was on the decline. How conscious he was when improvising is difficult to assess. But the outlet was considerable and helped immensely towards his development.

In the following improvisation, he begins by asserting himself in the opening on two large cymbals. Then he lets himself go in a most poetical way. The whole piece is relaxed and spacious, first at a moderate speed, which then increases and decreases gradually. His choice of instruments is imaginative and competent. My part followed all his suggestions and never prompted anything, but he still asked for the musical support it gave him. The improvisation does not come to a conclusion, it fades away.

Improvisation

Oliver: two large cymbals, glockenspiel, drums, small hand cymbals, chime bars
J.A. : piano

Third period

During the first three years of music therapy Oliver had acquired a number of skills, had absorbed a certain amount of knowledge which he could apply to different purposes. Moreover, he certainly had an innate need for music, a truly creative musical personality which had helped to give him a sense of identity and fulfilment. We were at the end of three years, on the brink of what might be called music education. The task was now to bring consciousness into the patterns familiar to him and to integrate them through the cognitive processes necessary to all constructive learning. In music, as in all other fields, the child has to transform into developing patterns the stereotyped or automatic knowledge he has absorbed. But it often happens that the autistic child suffers from a certain degree of mental retardation. Even if his islets of ability remain intact, they cannot always help towards an integrated mental process.

Oliver's progress in music had reflected and reinforced much of his general development in perceptual processes and awareness, in motor control, in his span of attention; his memory, his verbal ability and vocabulary had increased. He had acquired a sense of mastery and some confidence in himself. He was still a timid child but tried to communicate, to project and express himself when he was in a secure environment.

He had become more sensitive to praise and more aware of his identity. He now used the first person when he announced himself in the microphone before recording, and during the play-back when I asked him who was playing the drum, he answered 'me'. In music he had come out of the initial chaos into more orderly performances. He was also coming out of childhood.

The piano
At this time I tried to enlarge the field of his musical activities without spoiling the sense of freedom and independence or the sensuous pleasure he found in music. Oliver, like many autistic children, could handle complex visual stimuli if they remained in his field of vision. His orchestra fulfilled these conditions, and moreover the techniques involved did not demand complex

motor integration. His achievement here might have deceived a casual observer as to his level of intelligence. But an attempt could be made towards some intellectual development, provided that an exact visual cue was available at the time, and also that a specific sound was always produced at the same place. The obvious place for such an attempt was the piano keyboard, keeping to a restricted number of notes. The space was first limited to one octave, namely the eight notes starting on middle C. It corresponded visually and musically to the series of eight chime bars he was familiar with. For these reasons and also because of the suitability of his hands and fingers I chose the piano as the most suitable means to bring immediate reward. I hoped to introduce Oliver to the symbolic representation of musical sounds in writing.

He had begun to read words and liked the act of writing. I concentrated first on developing the independence of each finger and each hand. At first I placed my hand and fingers over his and pressed on them for him the feel the pressure of each finger on the key. The main difficulty in every field was in avoiding stereotypes once he had learnt something, and in preventing him from being confused by too many changes. Therefore I tried not to concentrate too long on a pattern which, once he had absorbed it rigidly, would create a barrier to progress. After a few months, he achieved the following result. This delighted his family who did not appreciate his improvisations. And Oliver felt grand when he was sitting at the keyboard, using his two hands.

Piano solo

The process demanded from him a major mental effort of attention and retention. As he was beginning to read words, he could grasp the relationship between sounds and their symbolic representation. As he knew the alphabet I used the letter names of the notes and he sang them when he played. He learnt how to play octaves with both hands and acquired an excellent posture at the keyboard. He certainly enjoyed being at the piano and was ready to make an effort, but his span of attention was very limited.

I used with him my own metric notation system which is very successful with retarded children. He could now master a number of short rhythmical patterns, written down later in metrical symbols of duration. This metrical representation was helpful in encouraging him to hold his voice as long as possible, especially when drawn under his eyes when he was singing. Lines indicating the modulation of his voice on vowels had helped him immensely, and he could also draw them himself. (see Part 1 p. 18.)

Music and Movement
During the first period Oliver's physical apathy made it impossible to stimulate him physically through music and movement. He showed no reflex to percussive sounds, and strong accentuation frightened him. Nevertheless, I bided my time and as our relationship became more and more friendly and trustful we began to move together freely on suitable music. He became more and more aware of his body, his feet and his hands. He never initiated movement, but I avoided conditioning or automatism, hoping that he would become more spontaneous. As with all our other activities his inability to attend for more than two minutes at first created difficulties. But they rapidly increased to ten minutes or even longer. During the dancing he looked very happy, and sometimes he laughed to himself in a strange, remote way. There was no sharing or communication in his laughter, but he was conscious of me and held my hand very tightly. At first he did not initiate any hand movement on his own – he held mine and made it move. Only later could he move away from me and become more independent. After a year of moving to music he had learnt how to follow some easy steps of a country dance and could partner another dancer. He enjoyed it immensely and was ready to join a dancing group.

It was then decided to phase out Oliver's individual sessions he had had with me privately for several years. He was asked to attend the sessions I was giving to a group of autistic children in a hospital, which included a dancing group. There was no sudden break as I was there with the group, but our one-to-one relationship had now to be shared with other children.

At the hospital the instruments were not as many or as varied as mine, but Oliver could now enlarge his musical horizon and met other music therapists. He had opportunities to see and hear many other instruments such as flute, guitar, violin, viola played by expert musicians, who joined him in his improvisations. In the dancing group he had great difficulty in relating to the children, as many of them were younger. But he had been trained well enough to dance adequately and integrate socially. Later on he joined a strumming guitar group of adolescents playing pop music.

Music therapy had led Oliver to the enjoyment of musical activities with his peers. He had also acquired the ability to listen attentively to music, and could now discriminate between and relate to familiar sounds. His life was made richer by music.

PAMELA[1]

Pamela was six years old when she was referred to me for music therapy by the county medical authorities. She was an attractive, lightly-built child with small features, very blond hair and a squint in her eyes. I noticed that she had very powerful hands, almost aggressive. Her parents had adopted her when she was a few weeks old and they had no other child. At first she looked normal, but they had become increasingly aware that she behaved in a strange way, as if she had no contact.

They were utterly devoted to her and sought medical advice whenever possible. But little seems to have been done until she was near school age. She was then diagnosed as sub-normal with autistic features, the autistic features becoming increasingly obvious.

[1]   J. Alvin: 'Musiktherapie mit einem autistischen Mädchen', *Journal der Deutschen Gesellschaft für Musiktherapie*, 1. 2. 1973, pp. 27–32.

The parents were teachers and lived in a pleasant house. The child was brought up in a cultured environment and well cared for. The mother told me that Pamela could utter a few isolated words and understood a few simple sentences but could not converse. The parents gave me their full co-operation which greatly helped towards the progress of the child. The father drove a long way to bring her to me and attended all the sessions for several years.

Shortly after beginning the music therapy sessions, I went to the Centre which Pamela attended every day. I wanted to observe her behaviour among children and adults. It was what I had suspected. The Centre (now a special school) was well-equipped with a devoted staff. Most of the children were severely sub-normal, not autistic. Pamela was unable to relate to any of them or even to the staff. She scarcely joined in any of the activities and showed no interest in anything the Centre could offer her. She could handle bricks with a certain manual dexterity but with no sense of purpose. She became totally absorbed in dabbing paint on a large piece of paper, oblivious of the people around her. She would suddenly abandon what she was doing with no sense of achievement. She sat at the piano alone, pushing away any child coming near the keyboard. She did not communicate except through refusal or resistance. Nevertheless, although our acquaintance was very recent, she recognised me and said my name after some time.

Before seeing her I was told that 'Pamela is most interested in music, spends much time at the piano, and on hearing any form of music from radio, television, and tape recorders she shows an immediate response. If she were to enter a room with a piano it is the first thing she would go for.'

First period

Pamela's behaviour showed many of the well-known autistic symptoms. When she entered my music room, she seemed to be oblivious of the surroundings, absorbed in herself. She went round aimlessly, touching briefly various objects one after another, and seemed to have no contact with any of them. She was shut in a world of aloneness, held her head down and kept her eyes averted, but could perceive everything in the room. She seemed not to hear when spoken to; she looked through me, not at me. Even her smiles seemed to have a secret meaning and were not a means of communication.

Little by little her autistic symptoms became more apparent. She had a few mannerisms of hands and fingers, seemed to avoid direct contact with objects through her finger tips or the palm of her hand. She scraped the strings of the autoharp with the outside part of her nails in a pushing-out movement, and did the same on the keys of the piano. It took her a long time to learn how to pluck a string with a finger or to feel the piano keys under her finger tips.

Her feet seemed to have no direct contact with the ground. She bounced or hopped instead of walking. She reacted to sounds in two extreme ways. Either she became silent and totally involved, lost in the vibrations of long, harmonious sounds, or, when hearing loud, stimulating and fast sounds, was seized by a kind of frenzy, making uncontrolled, rapid movements, flapping her hands, wrists and feet and grinding her teeth furiously.

Pamela's main autistic symptoms were her aloneness, her fierce resistance to any kind of penetration which called for a response, her need for sameness. She resisted violently any change of any kind in her established pattern or ritual. She was hiding behind an autistic wall which was both a refuge and a prison, guarded by a number of defence mechanisms which included eye avoidance, manipulation, temper tantrums, elective mutism or deafness.

A close observation of autistic children's responses to music often reveals that although the sounds may penetrate, they do not elicit a communication from the child. Sometimes, even, music seems to reinforce the process of isolation and thicken the wall between the child and the outside world. A musical experience can help most normal people to escape from the environment in a healthy way. But to a child already cut off from the outside world the uncontrolled use of music may prove to be inadvisable or even harmful unless it is an experience of perceptual and conscious reality. Love of music may offer the child a pathological means of getting involved deeper and deeper in himself.

Pamela, when humming, singing or playing music seemed to be wrapped in her own sounds through the web they created around her. I had to break into her world of musical aloneness, to make music become a two-way means of communication between her and reality, to make it become a conscious relationship, an experience at the same time positive and creative.

At the beginning Pamela resisted fiercely the sharing of a musical experience. When I attempted to sing or to play with her, she pushed my hand or my fingers away from the instrument. She treated my finger as an object not belonging to a person, and tried to get hold of it and throw it away. Sometimes she used it to strike the keys. When she was at the keyboard she did not seem to be aware of anything around her, unless, like my finger, it looked like something invading a territory which belonged to her.

Her security seemed to depend on her isolation, on the protection afforded by her symbols and the ritualistic sameness of the environment. Any change would provoke in her a temper tantrum. She threw herself on the floor, kicking and shrieking, during which time I kept still and silent. She was physically very strong, especially in her fingers which could break or bend anything resisting her.

As time went on, her obstinate will-power became more positive and more purposeful. It helped towards the development of her identity, expressed within a musical experience. She had obsessions related to musical activities which I had to break down gradually. For many weeks she was willing to take out of the box only one chime bar at a time and play on it. When she wanted to use another one the first chime bar had to be returned to the box. The sight of two chime bars together on the table provoked in her a temper tantrum.

I have seen other autistic children whose ritualistic number of chime bars was two at a time. None of them could bear to use a higher number until the obsession had disappeared. With Pamela the musical rapport between the sounds of two chime bars, namely an interval, could not yet be produced. When I attempted it, she snatched the beater from my hand as if she did not want to hear two different sounds. Her avoidance of notes producing an interval seemed to be related to her obsessive search for unison. The unison became the key of our musical relationship which led to a breakthrough two years later.

I observed very soon that she had an uncanny sense of pitch, one of these unexplainable gifts that autistic children sometimes possess. She could match perfectly and immediately on the keyboard or on her chime bars any similar sound coming from another instrument. She obviously had an intense, obsessive satisfaction in the perfect rapport created by a unison. She soon realised that other musical sounds she was hearing in the room were similar to or different from hers. She felt the difference as an opposition, resisted it furiously and went on repeating her note with insistence. She seemed not to be able to bear and accept the relationship created by the intrusion of another sound.

After a long fight of several weeks, she unexpectedly yielded and tried to pitch her own sound according to the one which I had just played. Thus she had adapted to an outsider and accepted the relationship it entailed.

At a later stage she would hear a rhythmical pattern in the distance and imitate it. At last she had become aware that she was answering an external message whose sound was symbolic of a presence somewhere in the room. During the following sessions I gradually moved up nearer and nearer until she finally agreed to share with me the territory of the keyboard and even the piano stool.

At that stage she often took my hand and used it to play on the piano notes similar to those of the chime bars, humming softly to herself. She also let me sit near her at her little table sharing the instruments. These were vital steps from which our relation ship progressed without any more rigid resistance, although Pamela still went through stormy periods of temper tantrums.

As her defence mechanism broke down gradually, her musical responses became more positively controlled and orderly. Her obsession for unison disappeared, but was replaced by another obsession when sitting at the piano by herself.

The piano is a self-contained piece of furniture, a kind of enclosure limited by wooden boards on every side and in which the player may feel alone and protected. I had noticed that Pamela always sat at the end of the left hand side of the keyboard, near the wall. This position might have given her a sense of security, or might have been dictated by her preference for the dark low sounds of the bass keys. She used her thumb and the first finger of the left hand to repeat an obsessive interval on the same two notes in a monotonous repeating pattern, with the emphasis on the semi-quaver.

Then she became totally lost in herself. I tried to incorporate her pattern in a free improvisation, but she seemed not to hear anything else but that. It sounded like a signature tune which could not be shared.

The development of her perceptual and social awareness, and even her resistance to certain experiences were a proof of her growing sense of identity which was developing in a non-threatening environment, in a room where she could hear and create sounds herself in freedom. I added a discreet part, mostly on the piano, to the short unfinished musical patterns she was playing on her various instruments, though I left her untouchable signature tune alone. The patterns consisted of series of sounds on the cymbal or on the chime bars, chords on the autoharp, glissandos on the xylophone and so on. My part on the piano consisted of a repeated bass, of musical questions or answers through which she could become aware of the sounds around her.

She used rhythmical patterns of an obsessive kind only on repeated sounds. On the piano her improvisations were more in the shape of an exploration such as in the following example, the two hands playing alternately, coming to no musical conclusion.

At this stage it was still not possible to structure or plan our activities, many of which were unpredictable with a child who oftensufferedfrommentalregressionsoremotionaldisturbances. But some musical order in her activities was established within a couple of years, and this helped towards achieving the ultimate goal: to use music as a means of penetration into Pamela's closed world, to make an opening through which she could communicate, express herself and develop her own identity.

Within a couple of years Pamela was able to put some musical order in her activities, which became increasingly satisfactory to her as a means of self-expression. We were still far from the ultimate aim, but Pamela was more able to project herself and to develop her own musical personality.

Her manipulative skills improved and her tactile perception increased gradually. So did her auditory discrimination. These developments helped to increase her conscious involvement and the immense pleasure she found in music. She became more and more familiar with the techniques producing certain musical effects of speed, loudness or frequency. She became verbally and vocally more responsive, probably because she felt she was gaining some mastery in a non-threatening field. Our one-to-one relationship had been steadily growing, and this included physical contact.

Since from our first meeting Pamela had tried to avoid physical contact I was always careful to hide my hands behind my back when coming near her – I also avoided any kind of movement which would have made her recoil. To many non-communicating children hands seem to be threatening objects. Pamela rejected my hands, pushed them away and would not let me sit by her. But when she had become familiar with the instruments which were intermediary objects and not threatening, she let me come near her at her little table or on the floor, and became more co-operative.

I had patiently waited for the moment when she would agree to be in close proximity with me. Then it became possible to begin moving to music, to make her aware of her body and discover the joy of physical movement.

She had no body image, did not even seem to feel her feet. At first she moved in a passive and uncontrolled way and followed me. After a few weeks she became able to do orderly steps, turns, spins, stops and even to move by herself. The spontaneity of a non-stereotyped use of her body was to her a revealing experience. She often laughed and looked happy when moving to music in an uninhibited way, but with enough support to feel secure. The support was chiefly in holding my hands. Then, as she progressed, she found direct support in the music itself.

She became aware that her feet belonged to her, to be moved with a certain purpose, such as walking, jumping or bouncing. She could not lift them properly or in time. Little by little I succeeded in making her aware of her knees, her arms, her hands, her head. She became able to walk forward and backward, holding my hands and feeling secure.

She learnt how to be graceful and even certain dancing steps with me as partner and holding my hands. She never showed any resistance to this kind of activity, and looked very happy. She developed a grace of movement, nimble and light. She was a pleasure to watch.

The music I used was non-percussive, with a flowing, flexible rhythm, provoking spontaneous freedom of movement. It had to counteract her rigidity of movement which seemed to correspond to the rigidity of her mind and set habits. Moving to music can be a liberating and total experience.

Her growing awareness of physical rhythm helped her to form rhythmical patterns in her mind, and she sometimes used them on her instruments.

At this stage, it was not possible to develop her singing voice. During the first month she had been able to sing very softly a small cradle song 'Sleep my baby' which she interrupted several times by loud incongruous outbursts of 'Goodbye Miss Alvin'. But her singing ability soon disappeared. All she could do was to hum to herself. During the first year, she learnt how to pitch her voice accurately to a given sound, but she could not repeat or imitate a melodic sequence.

The account of the progress made by Pamela during the first two years of music therapy is illustrated by the regular tape recordings I made during her sessions. She had grown up in every way, her speech had improved, she could control herself better. She had found in music a liberating force enabling her to express and project herself without fear. But she was two years older, and to an autistic child the passing of time is bound to raise new problems and create further need for help.

Second period

The following pages describe the event which led to a break-through in Pamela's general development and crystallised our relationship. From there, we could take a cautious, more educational approach. Although Pamela's behaviour was improving at the beginning of the second period, I wrote in my notes at the time:

Pamela seems to expect everything to come to her into her closed world, words, music, objects or sounds, without using them to project herself. She perceives everything in the room, understands words, hears sounds, but she seems to feed on things around her and to absorb them without using them in a normal feed-back process of communication coming from her, a process leading to mental and emotional development.

She behaves in this way with her musical instruments, seems to grab them towards herself, and to possess any object without sharing it. These objects are part of her territory, namely the keyboard of the piano, the row of strings of the autoharp, her space on the floor, the top of her table. She fiercely defends against any intruder her territory and the objects she has made her own in an uncompromising way. She is so involved in all the musical instruments that she scarcely notices the many other objects in the room.

At the beginning of the second period I noticed that Pamela's temper tantrums were becoming more frequent and less severe. She was going through a general period of regression, had lost some of the progress she had made, was tense, grinding her teeth more than ever, and her movements had lost their freedom and grace.

The regression seemed to be due to an upsetting family situation: the closure of the Centre, an illness of the father, and the mother being under tremendous pressure. Pamela had lost her sense of security, was negative, obsessed, shut up in herself, wilful and resisting. She tried to manipulate me against her father.

Her upsets were clearly expressed in the music room, and she had by now learnt enough to express them more openly. She refused some of the activities she had enjoyed, including playing the piano, was frightened of the cymbal or played on it without stopping. She would again play with only one chime bar and only on the floor. She stopped trying to match sounds.

I had to find new musical activities she would enjoy, in order to help her out of this bad patch. I offered her new instruments such as a violin, a cello or a kalimba. I tried to avoid too much stimulation and made her relax, lying down full length on the floor. I also tried to prevent any of our activities from becoming stereotyped and introduced frequent small changes. These did not disturb her sense of security or the continuity of our relationship. Her relationship with me became more stable as she came out of the bad period of regression. She began to know me as a complete person, to be pushed away or resisted if the need arose.

She became conscious of our one-to-one relationship and came to accept the sharing process. She was happy to lie quietly on the floor with me and to listen to soothing music. After some time we could work together at her little table, and if she resisted I held her firmly in spite of her wriggling and shouting, which I answered by shouting in the same way. At a later stage, when she was under some emotional stress, she found security in holding my two hands, clinging to me as if she were afraid of losing me. She could say my name well, in that strange voice which belongs to some autistic children. In the past she had sometimes used my name in an incongruous way, but now she related it to a real person and a real situation.

After the period of regression we could begin again where we had left off, and Pamela's musical achievements progressed steadily. Her musical improvement reflected and often reinforced her general progress, including the development of her personality.

Her fierce independence helped her to explore freely the technique of some instruments, usually searching for pleasurable experiences through sound. She would take the autoharp near the piano keyboard and try to match two identical sounds made by pressing on one key and plucking one string.

She was cautious, but not afraid, when presented with something new. At first she would not touch the violin I showed her. But when she was more familiar with it she pushed my hand away from the strings in order to have it all to herself. Ultimately she became quite skilful at plucking the strings and screwing up the tuning pegs. She also enjoyed using the bow on a cello.

She personalised the instruments she could handle. She said 'Goodbye sound' when putting them to sleep. Indeed her relationship with the large orchestral cymbal disclosed many of her musical affinities. She seemed to have identified little by little with the instrument, an identification which led to a number of musical and psychological developments.

For the first months Pamela had been afraid of the loudness and the size of the cymbal placed on a stand. I had not removed it but covered it with a large cushion. She knew it was there, but safely out of bounds.

She also had two small hand cymbals she was not afraid of. They were hanging on a stand and she used them freely and very softly. Sometimes when she was playing them, if I made a faint sound on the large cymbal, she stopped and went to her father saying 'sound'. I repeated the experience during the next few weeks until she did not seem to be afraid any more. She went on playing very softly on her own cymbals, until I noticed one day that she was hitting them much harder, louder and louder, and at the same time making loud vocal noises. She seemed to be ready to open up and express herself through loud sounds. I tapped lightly on the large cymbal, answering her sounds. This produced a breakthrough. She advanced with caution from the distance and came near the big cymbal which I had left out. She hit the cymbal with her beater and retreated immediately she heard the sound. Then she hopped frantically as she always did when she reacted to a strong resonance, but instead of retreating she stayed there. Little by little she began to explore the instrument, advancing nearer, trying various techniques with different kinds of beaters, or striking the instrument with the palm of her hand or her fingers. She tapped it on the top or underneath, watching it intensely, and responding at the same time to its vibrations.

She came nearer and nearer, got hold of the cymbal and after having carried it to her own place among the other instruments, she went on playing on it. Her investigation lasted for more than 20 minutes. At the end, she carried the cymbal near the piano and began to play on the two instruments in turn as if she were comparing or matching the two kinds of sound.

Pamela came to terms with the cymbal. It had become part of her zone of safety, a member of her orchestra. She was able to tolerate and then to enjoy the fullness of its sounds, which she learnt how to control herself from very soft to very loud without getting into a frantic state. Sometimes she danced round the cymbal in a ritualistic way, but kept well in control.

When she went through a bad period her relationship with the cymbal was affected in two opposite ways; either she kept away from it, or it was the only instrument she would use. I left her free to cover or uncover it with the cushion. The cymbal was often the centrepiece of the orchestra; she placed around it a number of drums and small cymbals and played them in turn. She played them quite rhythmically. She was not obsessed by them and could listen to other sounds played by me. In the end, we played dialogues, as distinct from duets, the most simple form being as follows:

Dialogue

Pamela: cymbal

J.A. : drum

Nevertheless, many of her former obsessions and autistic symptoms persisted. I tried to transform them in some purposeful way. For instance, I made her turn her two hands in a rapid revolving movement when she was about to flap them. I said 'turn hands' just before the unwanted reflex would occur. She became conditioned well enough to do it without being prompted.

Her obsession for her signature tune continued. It was an extreme form of musical autism, and could never be integrated into any musical experience as a means of communication.

The only way I could fight against it was to take her away from her place at the end of the keyboard and to make her play on the whole keyboard with both hands and extended arms. The use of space anywhere and in any form is one of many techniques that can be used with autistic children. The extended use of the keyboard where Pamela could perceive her hands and her fingers enabled her to do some finger work at a specific place and use distances to produce certain intervals with various sounds. The five-finger movement brought a marked improvement on the former use of the keyboard, when she had played safe. To a lot of autistic children the keyboard is a vast space, and as such may be fraught with dangers. The child finds it safer to play each key in turn up or down and not to skip one, as this would leave an opening in the continuous series.

Pamela had now got over this obsession. She was exploring the piano by herself She seemed to be searching for something, and used the pedal frequently, but she did not achieve anything artistic or sensuous. Nevertheless, she was certainly expressing something of her own and she related to musical activities with obvious pleasure.

She seemed to find a certain satisfaction in making an intellectual effort, and did not mind the five-finger exercises which gave the series of sounds a perceptual form. She became conscious of the pressure of each finger on the keys and could say at the same time the symbolic name of the note – 'doh/re/me' and so on.

As her father was trying to teach her reading with some success, I began to show her what musical notation consisted of: I drew a large stave of five lines and wrote under her eyes, near the chime bars, the three notes she had just played and said their names – 'doh/re/me.' Then I took her hand and traced the notes, singing the three syllables in turn. She could not copy any pattern, and just drew a faint scribble when trying on her own. But she became able to sing the names of the notes when she saw them. Her response was very slow and often much delayed. But it seemed to work well enough to be related later on to her finger work on the keyboard. Auditory, visual and tactile perception could then be integrated. Pamela was still expressing herself in vocal noises, especially high-pitched ones when she was protesting. But she could modulate her voice much better, on descending intervals of fourths, thirds and seconds played on the chime bars, or helped by strumming on her instrument. This progress showed a complete change in her attitude towards the process of 'give and take' in music which requires a willingness to listen, to follow and to accept, as well as the ability to express oneself. Her improvement is obvious in the following dialogue where she projected herself freely on the autoharp:

Dialogue

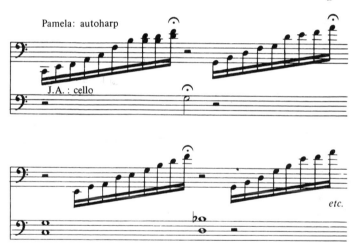

At the same time her speech ability seemed to be reaching another stage of development. She could say many isolated words related to the music and seemed to have conceptualised the word 'sound', which she used every time she heard a sound coming from any instrument. She had also learnt to recognise colours in her environment. She was beginning to say three-word sentences, not echolalic, but with meaning. For instance, when touching my skirt or a wooden surface she would say 'it is brown', or 'play the piano' when going towards the keyboard.

As time went on, month after month, Pamela's musical identity began to grow steadily. Her responses became more positive. Even her opposition was a way of asserting herself, and had lost its negative character. She was more conscious of the choice she made herself between the instruments or their use. Her activities had become more purposeful; she could stay longer on any given activity, sometimes 12 to 15 minutes. She had become more co-operative and willing to share with me space, objects or occupation.

Her perceptual awareness, her motor control and her auditory discrimination had developed. They enabled her to use different techniques aiming at different musical results. Still she had little sense of musical form or rhythm in what she did, unless it was directed and supported as when she was moving to music or when I played with her. She could imitate some rhythmical patterns she had just heard such as ♫ ♩ ♩. ♪♩ or ♩ ♫♫ She enjoyed orderly physical movements to music. Her body image was taking shape in her mind and she could use space freely when moving or playing without being frightened. But the girl still needed the musical and psychological support given by a structure or an environment around her. In the music room Pamela had sometimes been able to come to terms with herself. She had become less adamant. After her temper tantrums of which I took little notice, she often resumed her music quite happily and even seemed glad of my presence.

Pamela was a strong child in spite of her fears and defences. During the first two years she had built up with me a stable, predictable relationship. Our sessions had become better structured and more purposeful. We could assess our achievements however small, and look forward to further ones. Pamela's growing satisfaction and happiness during the music therapy sessions showed that they answered a deep need. But we needed more than a gradual development to operate a breakthrough and help Pamela to project herself. This came suddenly at the beginning of the third year, and gave the whole work another dimension.

Third period

The breakthrough which occurred at the beginning of the third year was a sudden event. It followed a gradual development in my relationship with the girl, from a total refusal to acknowledge my presence, to periods of fierce resistance, tantrums, withdrawal or regression expressed in fears, panics and conflicts as well as in her inability or refusal to come to terms with reality. Nevertheless, the music room was a zone of safety and freedom where she was accepted and could express herself.

She acquired a sense of musical identity, became aware of her musical needs. Her relationship with me improved immensely. She felt so secure with me that she did not need any more the presence of her father in the room. It is significant that the breakthrough took place when she was alone with me. Her horizon at home had widened. She had been riding a pony for some time, an activity which must have given her the close and direct awareness of a living thing. This might have been instrumental in the breakthrough with me.

On a summer day Pamela was alone with me, and as usual, after playing on the big cymbal, put the instrument 'to bed.' Then she suddenly rushed and jumped at me, embracing me, holding me tight. At the same time she was uttering rapid, joyful sounds and laughing loudly. I then said calmly: 'Now, what are we going to do? Can we jump together?'. We went round the room. Pamela holding me tighter and tighter. I held her up, made her swing and began to sing: 'Hop together like little ponies with Pamela who is a good girl'. She embraced me, laughing heartily, not in her usual psychotic way, but just like a normal child. She seemed to be under the release of a deep-seated emotion which was at last coming into the open; it touched me immensely. After a long time, she calmed down and still alone with me she went on holding me tightly and affectionately. We played together the autoharp and the drums. She said 'No' firmly when I suggested that her father could come in. The whole session was recorded and the tape is indeed a most precious document.

After that date the child seemed to become increasingly liberated, communicative and co-operative. Every week she repeated the same effusive performance, clinging to me and shouting, with delight such words as: 'diji, diji'. When we sat together at the piano, she now put her arms affectionately around me. Her behaviour became more and more outgoing and stayed so until she left me the following year.

She had gone a long way musically, her improvement was linked to and had helped her general development. She had acquired enough self-confidence to dance or move by herself when I was beating a rhythm on a drum. She became sensitive to praise and even accepted a challenge to do better. She did not any more avoid looking at me.

She became quite positive in her own choice of activities, not as an act of protest or rebellion as she had done for so long – although she was often stubborn, refusing to open her mouth to sing. She still expressed refusal by making small moaning, babylike noises or cries, but she could control some of her tempers. They became more frequent when she acquired new obsessions such as picking her nose. To counteract these, I added to the movement session 'touch your nose', and she could then use the action with a purpose. I began to use the cymbal as a conditioning device, and played a sudden loud noise on it to warn her against undesirable behaviour. She immediately stopped, quicker than if I had spoken. After a while the sight of my beater poised for a loud bang was enough to stop her even before the sound was heard.

As we were musically nearing a more educational approach, Pamela's reaction to a learning process became more that of a normal retarded child. I had to assess her actual state and judge how much she could bear the stress of a mental effort. She often manipulated me in the process, alternatively embracing me and resisting me.

Musically, she had acquired a number of skills, could use any of her instruments with a purpose and as a means of self-expression. She could use two hands independently on a drum or a xylophone. Her dancing rhythm had improved together with her awareness of feet movements.

The techniques on chime bars helped to stimulate her creative ability. She used them to accompany some series of words or numbers, accurately and rhythmically. Her squint had not prevented her from developing a good eye-hand control, which she demonstrated through using her sense of colour and her affinity for machines. We stuck some coloured stars on the large surface of the cymbal. She then called a colour herself and tried to strike the appropriate star with her beater. The process was more difficult when she made the brass circle revolve, or when she had to play alternatively loud or soft.

I also used the metronome to make her follow with her hand the movement of the pendulum, and often changed its speed. She called the metronome 'tock' and it was very much alive to her.

It is sometimes desirable with obsessive children to avoid stereotyped series of diatonic or pentatonic sounds. I let Pamela mix her chime bars in any order. She usually played from left to right and repeated the series in both directions, on various rhythms, usually ending with the starting note, which produced an effect of form.

Composition on Chime Bars

None of her musical achievements were obsessive or stereo-typed. The only field in which her obsession remained was in her use of the piano. When she was sitting alone in front of the keyboard, she disappeared entirely into her own autistic world. However interesting psychotic musical behaviour can be to a psychologist, the question remains whether it is wise to let the child find in music a means of isolation and a refuge from the world of reality, or whether music should be used as a means of communication and awareness. It may be possible to use both. I did not try to wean Pamela from something which had become a necessity to her. But little by little I made her conscious of the relation of a piano to the outside world. She became aware of the whole length of the keyboard and the arm movements required to cover it – of the finger work on the keys, and of the sounds made on the instrument and of their relation to other musical sounds. Also she accepted sharing the keyboard with me. The long-term process changed her attitude towards the piano but did not prevent her from using it sometimes as a means of isolation. The habit was too deep-rooted. The five-finger exercises mixed with other sequences she was familiar with helped her towards a technical achievemnt. It was orderly and purposeful and she did not resist it. I left her totally free to do on the keyboard what is called 'free improvisation', which, at the beginning, may consist of undirected movements all over the keyboard. But out of this chaos, some patterns usually emerge, are repeated and take form. Pamela's improvisations were unrhythmical and at times sounded like a never-ending search in which she was totally absorbed and lost. When I tried to break through she made baby-like protesting noises. She liked the sustaining effect of the pedal. Among the sounds she made one could detect many repeated notes played faster and faster but never rhythmically, which seemed to express aggressiveness or temper. Sometimes the sequence of five fingers was included. She had obvious pleasure in hearing the sequences she produced on the piano using the left and the right hand in turn. The form of the improvisations was indefinite, and their end unpredictable. They often stopped abruptly without any seeming reason.

Improvisation

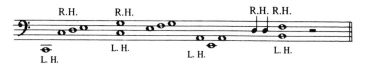

Pamela's singing had been hampered by her early regression into a 'no singing' attitude, her unwillingness to utter musical sounds or words in music. Nevertheless, during the last period she learnt how to sing 'doh/re/me' with the chime bars in a weak but pleasant voice. She also uttered pitched musical sounds when playing her instruments. But she went on refusing to blow a wind instrument.

Her improvement in speech enabled her to express verbally some of her wishes in the music room instead of using undesirable means to impose her will. She said quite clearly 'Want to play piano – put cymbal to bed – goodbye tock – choose a drum – goodbye sound'. She was still unable to use the first person or to converse.

At that stage of her development the little blond girl had gained a positive awareness of music and many skills through which she could express herself in a creative way. In four years, we had reached a rewarding stage.

Perhaps after having supported an autistic child for a number of years and opened to her or him a channel of communication, the real reward of music therapy is to have brought the child to a point where it can merge into a more educational approach, and is not an end but a beginning. But Pamela had grown up and was now leaving home to go to a faraway boarding school where there was unfortunately no music to bring about a development on these lines. Nevertheless, music had opened in this disturbed child a creative source which could be channelled in other directions.

3 A research project

INTRODUCTION

The research project[1] which is the subject of this chapter was undertaken under the direction of the consultant psychiatrist of the Family and Child Guidance Clinic, and the Head of a primary school. It was conducted on three autistic boys between eight and eleven years old. The aim of the project was to try to help the boys to integrate into the normal primary situation by means of individual assistance given by home tutors and a music therapist. The parents were involved in the project and received help or even treatment at the clinic. The general aim was: to help the children to recover their spontaneity; to study and develop their individual potentials; to help them to catch up with their delayed emotional maturation. The greatest flexibility of approach and methods was essential to the success of the scheme.

The children were attending school regularly like any other children. They worked mostly in the classroom and shared meals and out-of-doors activities with the other children.

The team involved in the project included the consultant psychiatrist, an educational psychologist, a social worker and a music therapist, as well as a number of teachers and home tutors taking charge of the children in the school and at home. The members of the team worked in close contact with one another and gave regular reports on the children's progress and behaviour.

The three autistic boys had been at the school for over a year when my work began. My part in the project was an important one, bringing in a new element, a new person and a new situation. The boys were first to work individually with me, away from the school room. At the beginning I met them in a large, bare room, with a video camera. Later on we were provided with a special self-contained unit in the grounds of the

[1] J. Alvin: *Research on Three Autistic Children*, British Society for Music Therapy (1976)

school, a well-equipped cheerful room with all amenities including a one-sided mirror.

Although we worked in a school, my primary aim was not to 'teach' music to the boys, but to use music as a means of development through which their identity could be integrated. I used music as an emotional, mental and social force of integration; I used it as a means of alienating the feeling of anxiety and frustration common to many autistic children. In the meantime I hoped that the results obtained through musical activities would help to reinforce the progress achieved in the schoolroom and elsewhere.

Provided I could develop with each of the boys a relationship of mutual respect and trust, without creating in him a feeling of dependence, I hoped that sound and music would be a creative and liberating force which ultimately he could use and control himself.

I planned a long-term programme which included the direct and spontaneous use of very simple instruments and of the voice. I gave the boys a free access to sound, its pitch and its volume, in order first to take away all inhibitions related to noise or social manners. But my own behaviour was cautious and guarded. As usual, the approach is first a physical one, during which the child takes you in and assesses you in his own way. I avoided moving towards him except very slowly, holding my hands behind my back, never trying to 'win' him. I sometimes even walked away from him and increased the space between us.

The room was prepared to use space, distance or direction according to the child's reaction, which had to be observed carefully, but in a seemingly casual way. I knew that retreat from the child could only delay or even spoil the relationship I was hoping for.

I prepared the room in great detail to permit the psychological use of a given territory through different stages. The plan was inspired by Professor Tinbergen's work.[1] Nothing was to be changed in the arrangement of the room, since a change in the physical environment might have produced the child's withdrawal or revolt. The arrangement was made in order to provide

[1]   E. A. Tinbergen: *Early Childhood Autism – an ethological approach*, Paul Parey, Berlin-Hamburg, 1972.

areas in which the child would feel safe, and to allow him to enlarge his zone of safety when he was ready to venture further out.

There were two tables at one end of the room; a low circular one which could be used freely either as a seat, or as a table or a low platform. The other table, about two and a half feet away from the round one, was of normal height, around which one could stand or sit down, thus creating a closer learning situation if needed. A large orchestral cymbal on a stand in the middle, equidistant from the two tables, seemed to form a neutral zone.

This end of the room represented a limited and divided territory, the boy's being the small circular table, mine the tall one. The two parts were obviously separated. The boy could feel safe with his table, or even guard it by sitting on it. I was not a threat when sitting or standing quietly behind the higher table.

The musical instruments were placed on the tables, set out attractively, and the boy could choose freely between them. His attention was focused on manipulating the instruments and no direction was necessary. After a while there was coming and going between the two tables; and the boy shared with me the whole of the territory. We began by standing or sitting down. After a few weeks, the sitting position became one in which I could show the boy how to use his instruments. The large attractive cymbal, standing in the middle, helped immensely towards the exchanges between the two tables. The other instruments were chime bars, a melodica, autoharp, several drums, guitar and hand cymbals; we did not use a piano. But I used a cassette recorder to play orchestral or dance music, or any piece suggested by the boys at a later stage, or for the recording of individual sessions.

The individual descriptions of each of the boys will give an idea of what I call working on 'equal terms', an approach which I hoped would be successful and form the basis of future group work. The place of music therapy in the project is described in the following sections through the stories of Martin, Kevin and Geoffrey. The three boys had very different personalities: Kevin, the obsessive, violent, manipulative, unreachable child; Martin, withdrawn, insecure, suspicious, ready to switch off when afraid; Geoffrey, agitated, tense, hyperactive, unstable, moody and frightened. Each of them suffered from the learning problems caused by autism. Moreover, they were emotionally immature and had no sense of identity. But they could understand and use speech and were socially acceptable.

Kevin was outwardly the most autistic and, at eight years old, the youngest of the three boys. He was also the most immature, and had perfected an admirable system of manipulation as a means of self-defence in any threatening situation. He could easily get away with it, being a beautiful, fair child, with large blue eyes and a pink complexion.

From an early age Kevin had behaved in a destructive way towards the home, attacking and tearing things around him. He was aggressive towards his mother, but related better to his father, who had been treated for depression.

Kevin showed intense jealousy towards his brother four years younger than himself He also had refused to have meals with his family until he was four years old.

At five years old Kevin was diagnosed as mildly autistic. Between the age of six and eight he was placed in a training centre for retarded children, where he scarcely communicated and did not progress, although the teachers felt that he was able to learn. The parents at that time were having problems with their marriage. The family doctors worked with them to resolve these and a significant improvement was achieved. It was agreed not to hospitalise Kevin but to send him to his present junior school. When I first saw him he had achieved a reading age of six. At home be had stopped tormenting his young brother. There were no other children.

First period

In a musical situation, alone with me, Kevin displayed a number of well-known autistic features: sitting on the floor at the window, looking out, aloof and silent, impervious to any sound, noise or movement. He looked through you or gazed absently at objects, was obsessive and rigid. He seemed to be full of conflicts which erupted suddenly in a temper tantrum when he was contradicted. He wandered round the room, sometimes hiding himself. When he wanted to be left alone he flopped down on the floor with heavy limbs and could not be moved.

His contacts with me included a refusal to co-operate, escaping or resisting. Sometimes he did not mind physical contact, sitting on my lap and being coddled, but keeping aloof. He took all opportunities to suddenly pinch to the blood my thighs or my arms, a sign of aggression which has persisted for years, sometimes under seemingly affectionate gestures. He also kicked me violently when in a temper. At a later stage he tried to make a hole in my skirt with a stick saying: 'Your skirt is too large and too long'. All these attacks seemed to be directed against resilient surfaces, against objects or people who could or did not retaliate.

At the beginning he needed more noise than musical sounds, using his full strength against a large orchestral cymbal, or against drums whose surface is a resilient skin. He could not pinch them, but he pressed on their surface forcibly with his thumbs or tried to pierce them with a stick. He also pressed violently on the keys of the melodica, blowing it as hard as he could. All his movements were violent, obsessive, set against the resistance of the instruments. Little by little he learnt how to control them.

His aggressive feelings were mostly in his thumbs and could not be transferred to the whole hand. But a complete change occurred when he was persuaded to use the drums in a more musical way, namely in tapping on them with his finger tips and using a flexible movement of the wrist – and also in using his whole hand to produce an alternate soft or loud sound. The purposeful tapping of a rhythm on the drum, such as ♫ ♩ , helped to take away his obsessive pressing of the thumbs.

As time went on, Kevin's aggressive feelings came out only during the last part of the session. We could spend the first ten minutes on better structured musical activities, mostly on the chime bars and sitting together at the table. We sang his name, or short sentences including his name, on various melodic or rhythmical patterns.

He achieved a good command of the rhythm ♫ ♩ which I

did not allow to become obsessive. He possessed good finger control on the melodica, excellent eye-hand control and independence of arm and hand movements, a good singing voice and a memory for tunes. All this was musically promising.

Kevin used the melodica, the drums and the cymbal with pleasure. At first he did not take to instruments requiring tactile sensitiveness, such as the autoharp. But after ten weeks, when his defences started to crumble, he began to enjoy playing it, improvising singing tunes on it. Then real music came out of Kevin's voice and his strumming of chords with a good rhythm. This was part of a general development.

But Kevin's progress depended on his relationship with me. I had to create a situation in which he would lose his babyish manipulative behaviour resulting from a deep sense of insecurity. Kevin was a frightened child who needed help, perhaps in spite of himself, in the form of resistance to his attempts to escape or to dominate.

His manipulation expressed itself in grins, smiles, affectionate gestures, escape, silences, elective deafness to voice or sound – his own defence against penetration. He often pushed or kicked me in a sly, indirect way. Only once did he come out openly in revolt by spitting hard in my face when I was clearly refusing to be manipulated. To his great surprise, I said nothing and took him, unresisting, by the hand to get a handkerchief in my coat pocket. Without saying a word I made him wipe my face. He seemed to be stunned by my silence. This event produced a considerable improvement in our relationship.

I had to take into account his phobias and obsessions, some of which he acquired during the music sessions. One of them was about a long red scarf I wore and which attracted him. It became a fetish and a ritual. He could not begin his music without wearing it and was deeply disturbed if I did not bring it or brought another one. I did not wish to provoke a conflict related to the object, but I transformed it into a plaything. I put it round his neck or his waist to make him follow me when we were moving to music – I used it to blindfold him when we were playing at hitting drums. Little by little, the scarf lost its fetishist character and gained a sense of playful purpose. Then Kevin forgot about it.

During the following months, the various developments in our relationship became stabilised. Kevin was feeling more secure with me and with the situation. Fear had been replaced by a kind of familiarity and trust in a predictable person. He could to a certain extent bear the slight demands I made on him for discipline and for a mental effort. We often sat in close proximity, at the table, which was more or less a learning situation in a restricted space, or on the floor, which was a play situation.

I used all the activities possible in the play situation which corresponded to Kevin's immaturity: hiding in the room, pursuing or challenging him, using all the space available and the musical instruments. The standing cymbal sometimes provided a central focus and gave a sense of direction. We also began moving to music.

Movement to music provided a one-to-one relationship as close as one could wish. Kevin did not resist being touched. When we moved together to smooth music, I tried to make him aware of his hands clapping a rhythm, of his feet, his knees, pushing him forward and backward, making him spin. He enjoyed it, but the activity revealed much of his physical inadequacy. He bounced instead of marching. He stood cross-legged in an awkward unbalanced position. When I made him lie on the floor and blow in his melodica, he was quite unable to extend his legs straight. As he seemed to possess an awareness and control of the upper part of his body, I tried to correct this inadequacy through movement to music or play techniques involving the lower limbs. The play techniques adapted to his immaturity helped to counteract Kevin's detence mechanisms and some of his obsessions. They offered him a liberating, non-threatening channel of self-expression. But music itself was still a potential to be explored through a slow development.

Second period

Kevin's relationship with me developed along the same lines as during the first months of music therapy. It became more positive. Communication was often of a challenging kind. His eyes lit up when he was about to manipulate or oppose me, and he looked at me straight in the eyes or sideways for a brief moment. In time the situation became a playful one and lost its aggressiveness.

When he was sitting on my knees he applied with his body the same pressure he used on any resilient surface, even pressing on my feet with his own. I took this as a means of communication. But when he was angry he changed his behaviour and pinched my arms to the blood quite unexpectedly. This usually happened when I tried to ask him to make a mental effort, or to behave better.

His intelligence showed in many small but significant ways. When he realised that he had done something well – for instance played a correct series of a few notes on the melodica, he immediately followed it by doing the same thing wrongly and seemingly on purpose. His moods were changeable and if his suspicion was aroused, he became aloof. In music, he jumped from one thing to another, standing or sitting, all in a disorganised way. Nevertheless, he quickly learnt how to use the instruments at his disposal, and could sing better. He had a great pleasure in letting out his feelings, through the use of his voice and the instruments.

But as our relationship improved, Kevin was more willing to accept a learning situation in which he had to sit down at a table instead of standing or walking about in the room. He could now accept from me some physical restraint when he tried to get away.

There was no musical progress to be expected in a short time. During the first period of several months, Kevin's music therapy was part of a whole situation at school, which Kevin had to accept. Until this was achieved it would have been fruitless to try to develop the musical potential.

The whole situation had to deal with Kevin's behaviour and learning problems, which were linked together in a frame of stereotyped mental and emotional rigidity. This state made Kevin resist fiercely any change in his environment. At first music provided him with the safe, therapeutic outlet he needed so badly. Ultimately this outlet had to be controlled within a frame of action and development in order to become real music. From the very beginning Kevin knew that he could express

himself in the safe environment of the music room, and find
instruments on which he could freely project his feelings. At
first his reactions were more physical than emotional. Later on
he let out on his instruments compulsive and aggressive feelings,
and tumultuous conflicts in which I myself could be the protector
or the adversary, the silent witness or the friend or just a
presence – but never a danger.

Kevin's autistic behaviour showed in his obsessions, his
compulsive or aggressive handling of objects, or his refusals.
Frustration produced in him a state of panic and temper tantrums.
I always tried to make a purposeful use of anything new in order
to prevent its use from becoming stereotyped or ritualistic. It
was bound to happen during the first week, as it did in the case of
the red scarf.

Kevin was intelligent and perceptive enough to react normally
to certain situations during which I tried to make him face
himself and come to terms with reality. In spite of the pleasure
he experienced in the music room, even there it took a long time
for him to bear frustration with me. If he tried to come into an
open conflict with me, I retired to a corner of the room,
occupying myself with a small task. I treated some of his
tantrums as normal occurrences. Kevin felt that the music room
was a safe place where he could express himself without sanctions.

If during a temper tantrum he threw himself on the floor,
shrieking and kicking, I usually stood silent and watched him.
When he was calming down I offered him a handkerchief to
blow his nose and wipe his tears and showed him affectionate
concern. Then we resumed our music in peace.

During the second year he went through a major temper
tantrum which amounted to a test of our relationship. I opposed
him openly in refusing to adopt in the music room the unchange-
able pattern he was accustomed to when singing in the classroom.
He could not bear to have the music sheets anywhere else than
pinned on a board from which he followed the words with his
finger in a compulsive way. When I refused he fell on the floor,
screaming, kicking but did not attack me. My silent resistance
was stronger than his tantrum, which at last came to an end. It
had made him come to terms with the situation and himself.
From then on he accepted changes in singing activities, standing,

sitting, at the table or on the floor, playing the autoharp or the drum instead of following the words with his finger in a compulsive way. From that day, Kevin learnt how to perform with more flexibility and freedom. His singing improved greatly, and so did his handling of the autoharp with which he accompanied his songs. He had absorbed a number of songs from school assembly in the morning and later on we began to record them.

Kevin, in spite of his behaviour problems, was an intelligent child, able to change for a specific purpose when not overwhelmed by an inner conflict. During the following period, Kevin's musical progress followed closely the development of his relationship with me, and of his awareness of himself.

Third period

The development of Kevin's identity had gone through gradual changes in his reactions to music. During the first period, there was no core to the activities. His attention or interest wandered from one thing to another, and he could not keep his mind on anything. He could not support any demands made on him. He was skilful in avoiding communication, in a definite, unhesitating way.

He was a solid child who reacted in a positive way to music, and to other situations. I felt that he was strong enough to come to terms with himself, and to face himself. This was achieved after a long time through music. I was increasingly able to make demands on him and help him to face himself in a musical situation. A typical incident took place at the end of the third year. He was playing the cello and suddenly had a fit of unexpected anger, and started hitting the cello violently with the bow. I said nothing and took the cello away from him. This happened twice and again the following week.

Again I said nothing at all and offered him something else to do during which he behaved calmly. This incident reminded me of a similar one when he spat in my face and I kept silent. Silence obviously made a great impression on him and even sometimes helped him to face himself.

The third week, when I gave him the cello, Kevin took the instrument readily, but to my great surprise refused to take the bow and played instead in pizzicati. This was very unusual. But it occurred to me that somehow Kevin felt he could not trust himself with the bow and avoided using it.

When I had met Kevin for the first time, his speech was echolalic, his mind confused, he was not sure of 'who' was doing 'what'. During the music sessions I had to present him with very simple situations and purposeful activities, in order to avoid mental confusion and his escaping into an unreal world.

Little by little music made him become an individual in a safe situation, where he enjoyed as much freedom as possible. The instruments were his to use as a means of self-expression. They were never used as toys, but as valuable objects, well-cared for.

The technique of playing musical instruments is related to the physical posture of the player. It can reveal much about the state of the autistic child, especially if he is withdrawn and self-involved. When he was turned inwards, Kevin had to be prevented from crouching over the cello or the autoharp or from leaning over the xylophone. When he was singing I tried to make him lift his chin and project his voice forward. The use of his voice helped Kevin to become aware of breathing processes. He learnt how to pitch his voice and how to sustain long sounds when singing or playing the melodica or the cello. Kevin's responses to music were impetuous and obsessive. But the creative impulses and the motivation they provoked certainly helped him to evaluate himself

His desire to sing a particular tune, to hear a certain piece of music, to play on a specific instrument was urgent and rigid. He could not wait, lived in the immediate present like a very immature child. I often used his strong motivation towards a musical goal to offer it as a reward, provided that he was willing to wait and to control himself.

I also insisted that he should say 'I' when speaking about himself. So far he had always used the third person. He was very clever at manipulating and avoiding the issue, saying for instance '. . . play the drum' and avoiding the pronoun. But I never gave way and answered his wish only when he had said 'I'. He became less rigid and after several months spoke about himself in the first person. The improvement was permanent, not only in the music room.

Even at this late stage there were moments during which Kevin's behaviour indicated some conflicts or difficulties at home. Then he could use silent ways of refusing to communicate, such as eye-avoidance, switching-off or becoming unreachable.

Nevertheless, in spite of his resistance to change and of his manipulative behaviour, Kevin possessed a many-sided musical potential. He had a pleasant, natural singing voice which was spoiled by hard and rigid verbal accentuation. He showed a good response to rhythm in the upper part of his body, but none in the lower limbs. He often stood in an absent way with crossed legs and showed no awareness of his feet until his attention was drawn to them. But he had excellent control over his hands, arms and fingers. There were promising features in his equipment. But learning the technique of an instrument needs a certain amount of understanding of causes and effects and of their application. Manual dexterity is not enough. Kevin could handle a number of instruments instinctively, but without a purpose going further than the immediate use of sounds. He learnt a few disconnected things, such as the letter names of the notes on the chime bars or on the cello. He liked experimenting on new instruments and certainly took to the cello at once. During any session he had the opportunity of playing on eight different instruments and kept on those throughout the treatment, whereas the two other boys became more selective in their choice. Kevin's reaction to the sounds of the instruments he was playing was usually singing or a verbal rhythm. His singing reflected his mood and was an emotional outlet.

Kevin had by nature a beautiful voice, in tune and resonant. But it was spoilt by the words and the verbal rhythm he applied to the music in a rigid senseless way, without leaving any breathing spaces. I tried to make him sing his own words, and then to put some meaning into them. His voice became sweeter little by little when he could hear himself sing alone, not in competition with the other children. His rhythm when accompanying himself on the autoharp was usually good, except when he was angry or excited.

He acquired a good sense of dynamics, which he could apply on all the instruments. This was one of his best achievements.

He was sensitive to the mood of the music he heard, with a

good auditory memory. He could also beat time to the music when listening to it. He liked listening to certain tunes he already knew, especially when he could sing them at the same time.

The musical experiences I offered Kevin were based on extremes to which he could react positively. He achieved remarkable motor control in playing alternatively 'very loud' or 'very soft', in 'shouts' or 'whispers' on any instrument.

When he was rebellious or aggressive, his mood could change from 'shout' to 'whisper' and he calmed down accordingly. This happened especially with the autoharp where there is only tactile contact with the fingers and nothing to beat on as with a percussion instrument. The sound of the autoharp often made him hum or sing softly and his gentle side came out.

He was delighted and attracted by the pop tune 'L'Amour est bleu' which we used again and again in various ways. The flexible rhythm and harmony of the tune had a definite soothing effect on him.

After a few months Kevin's musical identity was growing. In spite, or perhaps because, of his behaviour problems he could be reached by music. He became able to express himself freely in music, which brought out his gentle side as well as extremes of aggression, revolt or panic.

He learnt how to control his fingers on the melodica and the amount of strength necessary to blow in the instrument. Later on he began to handle a bow on the cello, could remember the letter names of the four strings. His posture at the cello was good, usually relaxed, and his bow movements natural and flexible. When he was listening to one of his favourite tunes, he liked to play on the open strings and sing at the same time. Then his whole body came into action, and the activity gave him immense pleasure, integrating almost everything music meant to him. His bowing followed the rhythm of the music, the rests and the ending, showing how conscious he had become and attentive to everything involved in the tune.

Kevin's span of attention increased enough for me to relate the music activities to his lessons in the school room. Then I made use of what he had already acquired in the way of vocabulary or numbers, which I used in series of words or figures. He sang accurately and with a good rhythm on the chime bars the days of the week, the months of the year, the seasons, the names of the colours. He also used his own vocabulary imaginatively in short sentences. Even if the words were not always understandable he produced and sang such sentences as 'January is wet' – 'July is holidays' – 'December is Christmas', and so on. I applied the same technique to numbers and discovered that he could not recall how many sounds he had just heard. He related 'shout'or 'whispers' to loud or soft and to the movement producing the effect. But to him words and action were simultaneous, and he shouted the word 'loud' exactly at the time he was hitting the instrument. He could not say the word before moving, was not able to form a mental image of the movement and prepare it consciously. He could not, at that stage, be made to wait between word and action, a fact which later on would have created a problem in learning to play an instrument or to follow a conductor in a group.

As he liked the act of writing, I attempted to give him some idea of musical notation. I drew under his eyes the five parallel lines of the stave and asked him to copy each of the notes I wrote one after another. Little by little he learnt how to sort out the five lines and the place of the notes on them. I was hoping that in the end the process would take on a musical sense. But he did not or would not relate the process to the written work he did in

the classroom. He even refused to connect the two situations, and for a long time I had to hide from him the co-operation which took place between his classroom teacher and myself.

The self-contained occupation created by music seemed to bring Kevin a much-wanted sense of security. But to an autistic child any sense of security brought about by isolation can be dangerous. The danger of self-absorption in music seemed to be very much present in the boy, even when he was part of a group and sharing an activity. I observed this, not only in music, during the first few months, but for instance, when he was sharing a meal with other children at a small table and did not communicate with them; or when he was standing in the choir, singing and shut up in himself; or when he was absorbed and listening to a record as if it were an escape or a withdrawal from the world around him.

But gradually, great progress took place. Although at the end of several years Kevin was still living in a world of probabilities, the school provided him with a stable, predictable environment in which he had begun to develop his identity.

In the music room the activities he enjoyed made him conscious that he was there functioning as an individual, sometimes under protest, but treated as a real person, having his musical identity. And as there was no doubt of his love of music, Kevin's social integration could now be completed by joining a music group.

Social integration was finally achieved with two of Kevin's school mates, a boy and a girl who made music with him. I gave him the leading part which involved him in something with which he was familiar and reliable, namely singing and accompanying himself on the autoharp. The two other parts consisted of a steady beat on a drum and two chords played on chime bars. We began with 'Frère Jacques' and other familiar tunes. Kevin willingly accepted the presence of the other children and their musical contribution. It was a completely different situation from that of a choir in which he had no lead and no sense of identity. He also did accept fully my participation to his singing. This achievement was a milestone in Kevin's musical and social development, and he has improved steadily ever since.

When I first met Martin he was an eleven-year-old autistic boy, ungainly, with irregular features and a sallow complexion. He did not possess the good looks frequently associated with autism. He was timid and ready to withdraw and gave the impression of inadequacy and vulnerability. He seemed to suffer from pathological and chronic anxiety.

At the age of three, after a normal babyhood, his behaviour became compulsive and very disturbed, and his speech development stopped. He had fits of unexplained screaming. His behaviour created problems in the various schools he was sent to.

At the age of seven he was diagnosed as autistic with many psychotic features such as lack of affection for his mother, obsessions with particular objects, or with disaster or damage to objects in the home. His talk was compulsive, an incongruous flow of words. At the same time he became increasingly negative and withdrawn.

It was then suggested that Martin might be able to come out of his withdrawal and come out in the real world if he could find in it a satisfactory one-to-one relationship.

Furthermore, the many tests to which Martin had been subjected had shown that he was seriously mentally retarded. He had great difficulty in extracting and using information coming to him although it was thought that his disorder in communication might hide some higher potential. At that time, he was functioning at the level of a seven year old boy.

His background was stable, his parents were co-operative and had done well. It would have been regrettable if Martin had had to be sent to a residential home.

The clinical picture of the child is indispensable to the therapist, especially in team work. On the strength of that picture I could already plan for Martin a very general long-term approach. It would include a search for the various potentials which might be there, for ways of liberating him from his obsessive anxiety, of meeting his intellectual or emotional problems and of fulfilling needs which had yet to be discovered, especially a need for music.

First period

The way to build a satisfactory one-to-one relationship with Martin was first to deal with pathological anxiety, his continuous need for reassurance. His worried and questioning looks showed his mistrust of himself and of the world around him. The first day he came into the music room, he was wearing his outdoor coat and took it off only at the end. I made no remark about it since an overcoat often represents a protection to a psychotic adult or child. The second time, he took it off before beginning the session. He looked and felt inadequate, was easily frustrated, always afraid of making mistakes. I tried to give him confidence even before he went into action. Praise for what he had done had no effect on him. He seemed totally entangled in his distrust of himself.

The carefully planned arrangement of the room gave Martin a sense of protection. At first, all the exploration and sharing of music was done on the very restricted space of a small table, away from the larger and louder instruments which stood further in the room. After two sessions, Martin came in full of expectation and walked straight to the table. There we sat together in close proximity, side by side. Even when he came in carrying a precious fetish, such as a bit of string or a piece of wood, he felt so safe that he willingly put it out of sight in his pocket. He usually picked up the melodica first, which was placed on the table with other instruments. Later on I used two tables to enlarge our sphere of action and to enable us to use more instruments, increasing our musical territory until we could make use of the whole room.

Martin, on the whole, treated me in a friendly way. His difficulties were more with himself than with the adults around him. He seemed to have some social needs in spite of his sense of insecurity. His talks with me were one-sided and often incongruous, mixing fact and fiction, pouring out questions, never waiting for an answer.

A non-stop flow of words is a defence mechanism difficult to overcome. Martin's questions showed some interest in me, my car, my family. He kept on asking me anxiously if I would come next week.

He was obsessed by certain pieces of music related to television programmes. The social worker in touch with the family helped me to find out what kind of music they liked. This turned out to be the tune of the 'Pallisers' which I brought regularly for two years and which gave Martin the feeling that I would never let him down. His first words to me when I arrived were: 'Have you brought the Pallisers?'

I made the environment as secure and as predictable as possible, including my own behaviour, the tone of my voice, my attitude towards his attempts in music. But I avoided anything stereotyped, I changed things that were becoming too repetitive, without disturbing the familiar pattern through which he could learn.

Martin was a likeable, musical child. He loved the musical activities which we shared on what I call 'equal terms'. I never asked him to use or showed him techniques he could not apply at once and succeed, and I myself did not use other more advanced techniques. Martin's answer to any challenge at that time was defeatism and retreat. Before he tried anything he always said 'I cannot do it', even if he had been strongly motivated. Nevertheless, he could experience deep satisfaction in instant musical results. He became more skilful and therefore more ambitious, without the feeling that he had to achieve something at a certain standard.

It took him two years to express the feeling that he was 'doing well'. This came as a result of his involvement with the cello. At the beginning we shared the exploration of sounds made on various instruments. The most active 'drum game' consisted of a mutual challenge in reaching the other's drum, standing, sometimes pursuing one another and even shouting when the boy became excited and moved about. Then he lost his anxious look.

I had to follow his moods – often subtle or wayward – not always perceptible. His reactions to music always revealed his actual state of mind and could provide him with an immediate emotional outlet. On certain days he would not touch the cymbal or anything loud – on other days he would let himself go, hitting hard and shouting. In the room where he felt secure and protected he could enjoy complete freedom of behaviour. The relationship was as much with the music as with me.

At first we worked without a timetable, according to Martin's moods, his actual span of attention. But whatever happened, Martin's attempts were never assessed in terms of failure or success, but in terms of the pleasure he had experienced in a purposeful activity. The lack of strain and the complete freedom allowed Martin to reveal his musical personality which had come out spontaneously the first time he played the melodica and exclaimed: 'What a lovely sound'. Since then Martin had searched further for 'lovely sounds' on the autoharp and the chime bars. He could relate best to the melodica. This was an opportunity to make him conscious of breathing processes, especially when he tried to blow a long note. It helped him to sing better but did not improve his sense of pitch.

He felt deeply the effect of long vibrating sounds. This was reflected in his love for the full and flowing tones of the 'Pallisers' music. This innate love found another outlet later on in the cello.

Martin was typical of the melodic, sensuous child. He had no sense of pitch or rhythm or even beat, could barely clap his hands or move his feet to the beat of a march. But he was sensitive to a melodic pattern making sense. We often used the chime bars to sing his name or 'Good morning Martin' on a major third, or a sentence such as: 'Martin is a very good boy' on an ascending or descending scale of eight notes. He learnt how to do it himself and tried, although without much success, to pitch his voice on it.

Martin's mental equipment and training had given him a very simple concept of numbers. This helped him to acquire an awareness of individual fingers: 1 2 3 4   4 3 2 1   1 3 2 4   4 2 3 1, to be used on the melodica, and at a much later date on the cello, although at that stage any development on a stringed instrument would have seemed quite impossible. Nevertheless, I kept at the back of my mind the opinion of the psychologist who suggested that a satisfactory one-to-one relationship might help Martin to come out in the real world, and also that his difficulties in communication might hide some higher potential.

The awareness and control of breathing processes and of the voice can greatly help towards the development of identity and self-confidence. I tried to make Martin conscious of his singing voice, helping him to hold long simple sounds. As he was interested in numbers and measurements, I drew under his eyes a line corresponding to the sound and counted in seconds how long he had sustained his effort. He was much encouraged by a process he could understand at once which could measure an achievement and progress. It showed him that he was able to improve and increased his confidence and self-respect. The achievement was a reward in itself, assessed both in figures and in musical terms.

Tentative group work

After the seventh session and discussions with our team, I tried to make Martin work with two normal boys. This was only partly satisfactory as he was still immature and his moods were unpredictable. Martin was confused about his place in the group, did not understand what 'to lead' or 'to follow' meant. He did not watch the boys' performance and often opted out. Then he had to be brought back to reality.

He benefited only slightly from the active presence of the other boys, as an incentive to use the whole room in moving, jumping, running or shouting. Some of the musical group activities included those creating physical communication, for instance the sending of messages through the feet when lying on the floor. But the group experiment seemed to have been somewhat premature. Since then Martin has continued with individual sessions more suitable to the development of his own musical personality. He has other opportunities to work in a group at school.

During the first period I had been able to evaluate Martin's personality, to get a clear picture of his musical needs and the ways through which musical activities could provoke in him some perceptual, emotional and social development. But I was well aware that such developments would be extremely slow to give this disturbed and immature boy the fulfilment he needed.

This now depended on the development of our one-to-one relationship and on the way I decided to use Martin's musical potential, which was slowly coming to the surface.

Second period

Martin's main difficulty in life was his anxiety, his lack of self
confidence even in the most simple tasks, and which stood in the
way of his relationship with people. He was always seeking
reassurance, became confused if he could not understand, and
opted out of the mental effort required. All his contacts were
precarious. He was, as I have already stated, a vulnerable child.

After several months I had achieved with Martin a stable
relationship not affected by his moods. He found in the music
room a safe environment where he could express himself freely
and which provided him with an emotional, non-threatening
outlet. At the same time he needed the support of a structured
framework. This was provided by the order inherent in music.
The repetitive element in music is a support to the autistic child
so long as one can avoid the danger of its becoming an obsession.

On this premise Martin could trust me to encourage him
without pushing him, to let him work at his own pace, but to
expect from him as much as he could give. It was only at a later
stage that I began to stretch him mentally and physically, after
he had learnt to bear the emotional stress of learning.

He tried to relate and understand the world around him, a
painful process for an eleven-year-old autistic child whose reactions were so often incongruous. He was obsessed by his relationship with people, asking me incessantly if I were angry or cross
with him in spite of my reasssuring answers.

But his anxieties never came into the music itself. He never
handled the instruments in an incongruous way. He used them
to search and investigate sound. This searching brought out the
best in Martin as it was both an interesting pursuit and an
emotional one. It could, and ultimately did, lead him to learn
music.

In time Martin became more and more sure of himself.
Instead of doubting his ability to do something, he began to say
at the end or during the session 'I have done well', and he
became more sensitive to praise and achievement. At the same
time the easy challenges I gave him made him face himself
without fear and become more aware of himself. A musical
challenge may consist of repeating on a drum a rhythm just

played on a chime bar, or understanding the technique of playing 'loud' or 'soft' on a cymbal, or repeating the same note four times on a melodica – all of them are part of a musical consciousness and can be increased in complexity.

Martin's behaviour showed the way the complexity could be increased. Little by little Martin became aware of the meaning of four consecutive notes played with one hand on the melodica, then of eight notes played with two hands. As this achievement had made him ambitious, he challenged himself to play the series a given number of times without stopping. He asked me to write a series of figures as he was playing the notes. So long as we wrote down the numbers at the same time as he played the sounds, his patience was inexhaustible, and he always kept to the figure he had set himself, sometimes even up to 30, 40 or 50 which meant playing non-stop for ten minutes. This self-imposed task helped him to acquire excellent technical control of his fingers on the keys.

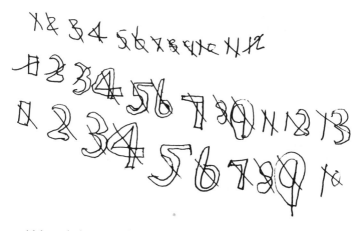

Although he was given complete freedom in music, using instruments, space and movement as he liked, it took Martin a long time to become independent. I had to give him musical, non-verbal support, in playing with him, moving with him, making him aware of the musical sounds in the room to which he could relate.

Little by little he developed more initiative, he could express himself more freely, he could dance and move by himself without looking at me for reassurance. It took him a long time to be liberated, self-confident and to experience the joy of creative independence.

The growth of Martin's identity has followed a continuous slow trend. He was at first an immature, hesitant, non-communicating child, obsessive and anxious. He often acted with me in an infantile way, keeping on undoing his shoe-laces or asking baby-like questions. His personality began to show and assert itself against me in an infantile manner, becoming openly defiant especially in the challenging way he used musical instruments. But this behaviour was not autistic: it was more in the nature of communication and of Martin in search of himself.

The barrier that Martin's flow of speech had created at first was subsiding gradually in the music room. He was becoming increasingly conscious of sound with meaning and expression – sound which included his own voice as it gradually improved through his voice practice. He had also become conscious of the social importance of speech as a two-way means of communication and not as a self-protecting monologue. His sense of musical pitch had been improving, and he had acquired a good ear for verbal sounds. In the third year he became aware of some of his speech defects and had a desire to correct them. He felt that they prevented him from being understood.

He became worried at not being able to pronounce clearly certain words such as: 'Cello, G-string, black sheep' and others which had taken on a great importance on account of his recent involvement with the cello. I showed him how to place his lip in the right position with the help of his forefingers, and to use his facial muscles. He was successful and showed himself to be teachable in such matters. He was delighted with the recording we made of his verbal progress during the music sessions. He began to use his voice more freely, hum the tunes he knew and work on verbal sounds he wanted to improve. Melodic patterns gave him the support he needed, for instance, when repeating the syllable 'I' on a tune he was playing on the cello. He did it on his own initiative.

I am convinced that in his long development towards self-awareness Martin was greatly helped by music. The many features of our music sessions seemed to become more and more integrated, and finally took a direction towards a great event in Martin's life. The impact the cello made on this anxious, disturbed boy produced results that could never have been foreseen at the beginning.

Third period

Mårtin's progress in music had been a slow process. The improvements were difficult to measure, but nevertheless the boy had to be made conscious that he was advancing in spite of the fact that his mental retardation was becoming increasingly obvious.

Martin's world was still often imaginary and unreal, but his fantasies were not a psychotic escape. They seemed to come from a distorted interpretation of actual facts. This did not happen in music.

Although his household and family were stable and supportive, any new situation affected his behaviour and his sense of insecurity. When he heard that he was going to move to a new school, he felt increasingly anxious, his mind became confused and it was more difficult to communicate with him. But this did not spoil or stop his actual involvement in music. On the contrary, I do not think one could overrate the importance of music and a cello in Martin's life, especially at that particular stage.

In January, Martin came up to me with a bright lively face and told me suddenly that he would like to play the cello. Nobody, including myself, could trace how this keen desire had come to him. There was no cello at the school, Martin did not know that I was a cellist. He told me that he had never heard one, but had seen a picture of it in a music book. He asked me how much a cello would cost.

The following week he brought me a school book with pictures of string instruments, and pointing at the cello, said: 'this is what I want to play', I was surprised as it was neither the smallest nor the largest in the picture. At that time his love of beautiful musical sounds was growing. He might have heard that the 'Pallisers' melody was played by the cellos.

I have met several handicapped children who had been emotionally struck by the tone of a cello in a recording and were longing to play it.[1] Martin was one of them. He was growing up and wanted to handle an instrument bigger than our usual ones. His request seemed to be a logical sequence to the work we had done in nearly two years. Martin kept on asking me how many cellos and violins I had in my house. His first contact with a real three-quarter size cello took place a few weeks later. I wrote at the time:

'I have never seen a child's face express so much happiness and satisfaction. For once, Martin seems to have no doubt about himself.'

From the first day Martin was able to remember the names of the four strings, to pluck them and even to start using the bow. In spite of his excitement he was physically relaxed and got a good idea of the bowing movement.

He could pitch his voice and sing the sounds when playing on the open strings as he had done on the chime bars. I treated him as a normal pupil and gave him a book for beginners[2] which was placed in front of him on a stand. He was ready to understand the symbolic notation of the four notes A D G C. All the work we had previously done could be integrated in the study of his cello. He began with the first page, using the bow or plucking the strings.

Open strings

This was to him a completely self-contained experience. Lorna Wing in her book *Early Childhood Autism* states that: 'an autistic child finds it difficult to watch other people perform and translate the movements onto his own body; he cannot

---

[1] J. Alvin: *Music for the Handicapped Child*, OUP (second edition, 1976), p. 6
[2] J. Alvin: *Cello Tutor for Beginners*, Augener

understand verbal instruction, but he can learn through feeling his own muscles move.[1]

Martin did not wish me to play to him, he did not listen or look at me when I did. He remained aloof and indifferent. Therefore I made him feel and move on the cello in the right way. If I spoke to explain something or to warn him against a mistake, it confused him and he asked me to keep quiet, sometimes angrily when he was confused. He identified with the cello, touched it all over, admiring its shape, the colour of the varnish. He had a dormant aesthetic sense of colour, texture and shape which he revealed later on when making pottery.

After several months working with the bow and plucked open strings, I made Martin use his left hand on the strings. He could easily relate the position and the movement of the fingers to the work he had been doing so patiently on the keys of the melodica. The connection between the two techniques made it possible for Martin to integrate in a concrete way his concept of numbers and fingering. The same applied to the visible length of the bow corresponding to the duration of a sound, a process he had understood by writing down a line corresponding to the duration of a sustained vocal sound and measuring its length on the paper. His progress was continuous but extremely slow, and little by little he mastered the second page of the tutor.

Bar and beat

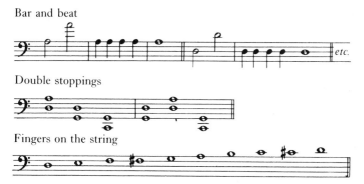

Double stoppings

Fingers on the string

---

[1] L. Wing: *Early childhood Autism*, Pergamon International Library (second edition, 1976), p. 201

At last he could play a scale in G major and a well known tune:

Martin certainly felt on safe ground when he played the cello. The foundations of this achievement had been laid from the beginning, and had matured very slowly. Therefore the tremendous experience that the cello represented to him did not create in his mind a state of mental confusion. The activities on the cello were orderly ones and did not make excessive demands on his mental ability. He added a cello part on open strings to all the tunes he liked to listen to on the cassette, irrespective of the strange harmonies which resulted from the process. He sat at the cello and played long notes with delight. This greatly improved his tone and his bowing. He also sang or hummed at the same time, moved his whole body or even stamped his feet. He could then experience the growth of his identity and maturity in spite of his many remaining features of autism including his relationship with people. He had several opportunities to demonstrate to visitors at the school how to handle a cello. He did it surprisingly well, with confidence and using the right words. But when he was demonstrating he seemed to speak to himself, aloof, looking down and not relating to the listeners.

At the beginning he did not seem to be aware of the results of his playing, let alone of their standard. I recorded his cello playing but at first he did not really listen to the play-back, not really feeling that it belonged to him. It took him some time to relate it to himself. Then it became very important to him. Martin avoided looking at himself in the mirror when playing; It seemed to disturb him, instead of being a source of satisfaction as it was to Geoffrey and Kevin.

Movement to music

From the moment I had assessed Martin's musical ability I had observed his total lack of bodily rhythm and his inability to perceive or interpret rhythmical patterns. This deficiency was reflected in the way he moved and in the way he spoke, both being disconnected and confused. He could not control his feet, he bounced instead of walking. He could not clap his hands in time, or move hands and feet together, on a beat.

It took more than two years for some kind of control to be achieved. Martin reacted very little to rhythmical music or to the stimulus of percussive sounds. His reaction was a gestalt one. He could not hear the different patterns which give music a structure. But little by little I noticed that he was sensitive to the general character and the mood of the music and that he moved accordingly. It became easier to play the kind of music he could be conscious of. This had to be done by means of recorded, not improvised, music in order to keep to the sameness he needed to feel secure, and use the same pieces frequently enough. In this way music provided a suitable background of safety which helped him to move with me and to be stimulated physically. Instead of letting him get hypnotised by the recordings, I made him react more positively during the music, but not yet to the music. This was to be achieved later.

I chose music at a suitably moderate speed and with a flowing non-percussive rhythm, which might lead to the use of movement. At first I had to guide him, facing him and holding his hands, even pushing him about. He never resisted physically. I used many of the usual tambour games, pursuing him in the room, trying to make him run, move his arms or his feet or even shout if I caught him. It was already demanding much from such a withdrawn anxious, suspicious child. I could not have done it before gaining his full trust.

He developed a good sense of movement, producing loud or soft effects on the cymbal or on the drums, but not related to rhythm. Nevertheless, on every occasion I played the pattern ♫ ♩ , and after a while Martin absorbed it unconsciously. Ultimately it became the foundation of his rhythmical sense.

From his uncontrolled use of physical movement Martin became increasingly aware of the physical pleasure he experienced when responding to the character of the music: bouncing his feet when the music was spirited, stamping them during a march tune, moving fast when the music was fast or loud. It was very difficult for him to synchronise feet and hand movements, to clap his hands and stamp his feet together. In the end he achieved it, but could not relate the movement 1–2–1–2 to the speed of the music.

At first he could not help his feet bouncing instead of walking, in a peculiar autistic way. He moved very clumsily, all in one piece. But soon he began to expand his movements, flexing his waist, spinning, using more space, extending his arms and visibly enjoying himself. Gradually I minimised my participation and let him move on his own.

The boy's emotional outlet when he began to move his arms freely was promising. He seemed to lack imagination, but given a theme or a picture suitable to the music he could function better and expand more. He began to move and mime a sea bird to one of his favourite tunes, 'L'Amour est Bleu' which provided all the requisites for inspiration and freedom. Martin used in this performance all the movements he had already mastered and added many others, for example an impersonation of a sea bird flying over the water, high in the sky, and diving down to catch a fish and eat it. It was by any standards a beautiful performance, and it was very moving to see the blissful expression on the child's face and observe his complete happiness. He repeated the performance every week, but it never became stereotyped.

From now on Martin's music therapy sessions included two main activities: the cello on which he had to make a substantial mental effort, and movement to music in which he could express himself in complete freedom.

Fourth period

Martin had matured physically and socially, becoming an adolescent. He had developed in many fields. His schooling had been successful, he could now read and write, his vocabulary had increased and his speech had improved. Altogether he functioned at the level of a child of nine. He had begun to learn to make pottery and to type. His activities at school included games, swimming, drama and group visits to various places. Perhaps his most rewarding performances were in music. One of his teachers wrote after attending one of his music therapy sessions: 'This was quite a revelation to me, showing how far Martin could be stretched: he was concentrating very well and trying hard on the cello. He thoroughly enjoyed the free movement at the end and really let himself go.'

Nevertheless Martin still encountered at school many of the learning difficulties due to deficient cognitive processes, to autistic behaviour, to an underlying anxiety when he was not in a secure environment. His infantile behaviour had not yet disappeared. But he was now able to take some social responsibility, for instance in making coffee for the staff or visitors in the unit. He was also good at supervising small children and showed kindness to everyone. In spite of this however, he was not yet ready to join a music group of youngsters. Martin was still self-contained and often aloof in the music room. There was in him a curious basic musical deficiency. He did not possess the instinctive reflex to percussive sounds which is common to almost everyone. He had to learn to feel the beat or rhythm that unites a music group. He would still have found a music group confusing and frustrating.

But he had acquired a real musical identity and had become ambitious, his world had been greatly enlarged by music. He danced quite often to Mozart's trumpet concerto, and told me that he would like to learn the trumpet. But he added immediately 'But I do not want to leave my cello, I want to get on with it.' His wish was not for a change, but for an enrichment of the musical pleasure he had already experienced. And he formed with me a lasting relationship far beyond our music sessions, which showed itself in many touching ways.

GEOFFREY

Geoffrey was ten years old when I met him for the first time. He was a good-looking, blond boy with nice features and blue eyes. He seemed to be small for his age, slim, physically alert and tense. The first impression he made of directness was belied by his sudden aloofness, the way he avoided eye or other contacts. His moods changed continuously, and his autistic behaviour took many forms.

He had been a normal baby for 16 months when he began to

withdraw and lost the speech he had acquired. His mother had already noticed his lack of response. At three years he was diagnosed as probably psychotic. At five years he was diagnosed by a consultant psychiatrist as emerging from a fairly severe autistic withdrawal. By then his speech had improved enough for him to be considered for a nursery or a primary school, but there his behaviour was so erratic and disturbing that he could not remain. He was sent to a school for malajusted children where his behaviour was assessed as obsessional, erratic and aggressive. He seemed to be full of deep-seated, bottled-up emotions and anger. He could not bear frustration. But he was already good at handling machines, including a tape recorder. A little later he was placed at his present school. He had one sister, two years younger. The family was close knit and cultured, the father a successful business man. They lived in a nice house and imposed a strict discipline on the children. They liked music of the classical type.

Geoffrey was an interesting and attractive child, full of conflicts and contradictions. On one hand, autism created in him problems of communication and social relationship. On the other hand he suffered from problems of learning due to his cognitive disability, which impeded the development of his musical gifts. These problems had to be either faced or bypassed. Accordingly I used the two approaches in the various methods I applied.

First period

A musical gift usually creates a need for music. My relationship with Geoffrey was based on the fact that he considered me first as a musician who could help him to fulfil that need. I had to find special unconventional methods to get over his mental difficulties and enable him to communicate with music as a means of self-expression.

In time we achieved a stable one-to-one musical relationship which set up a standard of performance and a spirit of tolerance. The one-to-one relationship became a one-to-four relationship when two normal boys joined our musical activities under my guidance. Little by little the group of three boys became independent and began to function as an entity. Geoffrey became part of a self-contained music group, able to manage itself and make its own demands on the individual.

During his first individual sessions, my main concern was to understand Geoffrey's problems and to observe how much of himself he could reveal through the music. Once I could judge how much or how little he could bear demands made on him, I decided to limit my demands to what was required by the music. I made no comments on his behaviour, however bizarre or excessive it was.

He seemed to be at the mercy of unpredictable moods, had sudden moments of opting out, or left the room abruptly, or did not answer my question, seeming not to have heard it. His eyes suddenly shifted away and he turned his head sideways. Even when he was in a forthcoming, buoyant mood, his state did not seem to lead to a positive relationship with me.

Music certainly provided him with a direct, emotional outlet. When he was contradicted, he became rigid and gave way to a musical tantrum, strumming furiously on the autoharp or hitting the cymbal. But he never threw things about, or destroyed any object or attacked me. At other times he would sulk like a young child, head and shoulders down. He seemed to experience the extremes of an emotional problem, oscillating between complete aloofness and forcible, violent outbursts. His face, and his body too, reacted to these changes by twitching or stiffening.

I tried to regulate his senseless, sudden outbursts of laughter, his uncontrolled flapping of hands, the incredible noises he was making when trying to be funny and to obtain a social success by doing so.

Little by little, his anxiety and loneliness came to the surface through the emotional outlet he found in a musical environment, which gave him freedom and a sense of security. I was able to build up with him a lasting one-to-one, non-verbal, purely musical communication through improvised musical duets. He has kept on enjoying them ever since, using his genuine musical ability and his imagination. We used various instruments to perform the duets, such as melodica, cello, chime bars and autoharp. I let Geoffrey make the choice for us both.

Geoffrey's reactions to music were flashy and impressive to an onlooker. His musical ability made it tempting to teach him in the formal sense. He possessed a splendid gift for projecting himself spontaneously. But he was unable to apply himself to a learning situation at that time. Therefore at the beginning I used a method which I call 'on equal terms,' where the teacher does not teach, but is a partner, freely exchanging parts on instruments, a method which gives immediate reward without imposing any standard of performance or improvement. In the process I tried to make Geoffrey conscious of his innate gifts. The first sessions helped him to achieve some manual skill on various instruments. His instinct made him choose the right sounds according to musical rules. He had at some time acquired a few principles of theory which he remembered, but they were disconnected. As he had been taught by his mother I wondered if his intellectual disability was not made worse by an emotional blockage.

'Instant music' can satisfy an immature child and works by an infinite number of means. Geoffrey's spontaneous response to this non-intellectual, non-verbal process was rewarding to us both and gave us a promising start. But in spite of this promising beginning I soon realized that he was not able to integrate the scattered, unconnected bits of musical knowledge he had absorbed here and there. His instinctive, imaginative musical gifts were elusive and his lack of cognitive ability prevented him from building up a core of musical knowledge. At this stage his inability and unwillingness to apply himself to learning came out. For instance, after three months he brought in a guitar he was supposed to learn at school in a group. He tried to strum the strings in an uncontrolled way and it was no good. I was told that he could not learn in the guitar class. He was conscious of his failure but seemed not to mind. When I offered him the autoharp to play on he took it gladly as a substitute. He used it skilfully to accompany his singing or to create an atmosphere with spread chords.

A musical gift usually reveals a musical identity related to the individual. But it did not take me long to detect Geoffrey's lack of identity, in music or otherwise. This was apparent in the way he continually 'acted out' another person who was never himself. He used to the utmost his incredible talent for imitating people he had seen or heard. This gave him the sense of identity he lacked. He imitated the behaviour of performers, instrumentalists, pop singers and others. This was an undesirable state of affairs, and had to be remedied for his own sake and for the sake of his music.

Second period

Geoffrey was musically gifted, but his basic learning problems stood in the way of a musical development. He had a good natural voice, he could stay in tune and in time. He could follow and sustain a given beat and control a rhythm. He possessed a rapid, superficial musical spontaneity. In spite of his slap-dash behaviour, I felt certain that Geoffrey could be deeply touched by a musical experience. Sometimes when he listened to or made music his face took on a look of repose and I thought that he had been reached. He possessed dexterity of fingers and good motor control. But his learning was mostly imitative and could not develop. His guitar-playing, for instance, was based entirely on having watched his teacher and the other pupils. He did not relate the technique to the musical result. He also imitated the teacher's singing as he did with pop singers on television. I understood that the attempts to teach him the recorder in a music group had been unsuccessful, probably for the same reason.

Our musical activities revealed some of his physical impediments. He used his voice badly, was unable to fill his lungs for blowing or singing, although he placed his hand on his stomach, imitating a gesture he had seen without understanding its purpose.

In the end his music-making was done on the instruments I had brought with me, which he said he preferred to those he had tried to learn, namely the melodica, the autoharp, the cymbal, drums and so on. These could be tackled in a non-intellectual, instinctive way and success could be achieved easily. Ultimately, Geoffrey did not continue with the guitar or the recorder. This did not mean that I discarded completely a more positive and constructive approach. On the days he was less tense and more open he could accept being put in a learning situation. We sat at the same table doing some written work. He remembered better what he saw me write down, and followed the musical symbols better when they appeared on the paper in succession.

He was not teachable when he went through a psychotic phase. He was shaky, flapped his hands, spoke to himself, mimed or mimicked, seemed to be unaware of his environment. He sometimes left the room abruptly like a rolling stone.

The use of the autoharp enabled Geoffrey to let himself go freely. The resonance of the chords sustains the voice without imposing itself and provides the incentive to go on. Geoffrey often sang a story he had invented, and which revealed many of his obsessions, his fears, his fantasies. He sometimes illustrated his story with extremely realistic noises or rhythms which he played on various instruments. The process showed his creative imagination in an unreal world. His lack of identity and his insecurity were all wrapped up together. He had an actor's talent for imitating other people's voices, but he never used his own natural speaking or singing voice.

His irrepressible vocal ability was greatly stimulated by music and gave him many opportunities to express feelings buried deeply in him. I encouraged him to tell stories in words when he was strumming the autoharp. The physical forward movement of plucking the strings very often helps the player to open himself and to lose his inhibition. We often recorded his stories. Most of them unconsciously revealed his insecurity, his deep seated anxiety. They told about a boy finding the door of his home locked – or being locked in a room, unable to get out – or about other people wandering round and knocking at unanswering doors. On some days when he was less tense or agitated, Geoffrey became more creative and orderly. He improvised humoristic songs about himself and illustrated them with realistic noises. They showed a remarkable musical gift and a feeling for form. But so far this gift could not develop further.

When I played Geoffrey's stories back to him, I had to make him become conscious that his own voice was not there, and he certainly knew it. At that time he had become aware that he had a voice of his own. I made it quite clear that we would record only what was sung or spoken by him with his own voice, and using the first person when he spoke about himself. I began a long period of conditioning on the use of his voice, stopping the recording immediately he began to imitate another voice. He was quite aware that I would not accept his impersonations. But even when he revolted, cried, or was near a temper tantrum, he came to terms with my decision.

We also recorded our improvised duets and I left Geoffrey in charge of the announcement, namely the names of the players and the title of the duet. Geoffrey said: 'Miss Alvin and Geoffrey D . . .' – or later on 'I and Miss Alvin', but sometimes the announcement of his music was unconscious or bizarre – a Beethoven Symphony or references to his family, nothing to do with the actual situation. He clapped at the end of his recording or made funny noises into the mike.

When we played duets I usually faced him, either playing the cello which was a positive object between him and myself, or placing a small table in front of him. He must not feel that I was too near, a precaution which became unnecessary later on.

Extracts from an improvised duet
(8 minutes)

Geoffrey: drum and melodica
J.A. : cello

His attitude towards me during the duets were musically straightforward. He chose the instruments, often signalled to me when he wanted to give me a lead, to stop or to go on. He always looked at me straight in the eyes during the performances. During the playback, Geoffrey got very excited waiting for the passages where he had done something special. When he was in a disturbed state he listened to the recording with flapping hands and made grimaces or funny noises. Sometimes he got very excited, and paced up and down the room reacting violently to any accentuation or change in pitch of his recorded voice. Sometimes he did not listen at all. In the end, he became willing to accept my criticism of the playback, although he was hostile to my commenting during his actual performance. Perhaps he felt no sense of self when his playing was heard in the playback in the machine, and the criticism did not affect him, but he liked the praise I gave when it was good.

Improvising duets with me, on any instrument, became the corner stone of our musical activities and of our relationship. He learnt how to control silences during the performance, how to listen to another player, how to take a cue. My part aimed at giving the shape and meaning to the music which were necessary for musical satisfaction. Geoffrey was musical enough to feel the completeness of the experience. Then his face really expressed happiness and release. The musical satisfaction he experienced greatly helped Geoffrey to integrate his musical personality.

As Geoffrey at that time was not able to be attentive long enough to fix his mind on one thing and acquire a positive skill, I offered him varied experiences and tried to integrate them musically as much as possible. When something interested him enough, I stretched him. For instance, we worked successfully on a five-beat rhythm applied to a number of musical activities. Geoffrey discovered that the five drums he was using were all pitched differently and made different kinds of sounds. He used them in a very imaginative way, especially when I added a part to make a jazz effect. He tried to make what he called 'funny noises' on all his instruments and with his own voice. I tried to integrate them in a musical context and make them purposeful. Geoffrey had a sense of humour in music. He often played a wrong note deliberately, then looked at me and said in his natural voice 'I am teasing you' and we both shared the joke and the laughter. It was a sign that Geoffrey's musical identity was developing and that he was taking the initiative in doing something against the rules and with a purpose. He could find his way on the melodica, for instance, in trying to play on it a tune that he knew. His crying need for success expressed itself not only in his making funny noises, but in imitating anyone who was successful, and he saw himself as a pop-star. He had an impressive collection of songs which were never musically accurate.

I made one attempt at that stage to make him achieve something constructive on an instrument which was new to him. I introduced him to the cello. On this he could have integrated his scattered musical knowledge, and perhaps experience satisfaction. This experiment was not a success. Although he had taken to it at the beginning, it did not last, as with so many other things one tried to teach him. He had no sense of working towards an achievement, and no sense of standard. He needed immediate, tangible results. His comment on his efforts on the cello was that he was making 'some horrible noises'. When I was trying to make him relate what he already knew in the theory of music to what he was doing on the cello, he could not do it. He could not apply to the cello the signs of crotchets or minims he had learnt in another situation. In the end the cello was used in group work by the group of three boys, to provide some effects of tone colour, or by me playing a leading part.

So far, Geoffrey had not shown any real ambition to achieve a mastery over any of our activities, but the benefit of his music therapy was to be found in another way. It lay in the freedom he had to express himself and use spontaneously his innate gifts for music. In order to do this and to produce a satisfactory, although a non-lasting, musical result I had to build up a lasting relationship with him, based both on his freedom and on my authority. He knew that I was willing to accept his infantile behaviour, his aloofness, his silences when spoken to, his leaving the room abruptly.

He liked his music sessions and often asked to stay on, sometimes for one and a half hours. The emotional release he experienced seemed to prevent him from getting tired. He seemed to view me as a predictable person and a musician, but there was no apparent feeling of love or aggressiveness towards me. The growth of our relationship was based on the equal sharing in the improvisation sessions. It made it easier for Geoffrey to accept my musical authority when I wanted him to make an effort. I could in the end make positive demands on him in spite of the freedom and choice that he enjoyed. I insisted that we stayed in a positive world of action and perception, touching instruments, watching and listening to one another with no opportunity to switch off. I think that the genuine satisfaction Geoffrey experienced was due to the creative, unconventional nature of the duets which involved a shared pleasure, co-operation, attention and freedom of expression.

But the duets were not the only means through which Geoffrey expressed himself. His amazing memory of pop songs provided him with a full emotional outlet, an outlet which the family would not accept as it was to them 'bad music'. He sang them freely and accompanied himself on the autoharp. The autoharp was an instrument providing instant success and a substitute for the guitar, on which the boy had miserably failed. It gave him the opportunity for rhythmical strumming essential to the interpretation of the songs. The technique did not require mental effort; it was based on memorised imitation and needed some manual dexterity together with innate rhythmical ability. But, in spite of his auditory faculty being actively engaged, the process did not lead to any coherent learning until it was used in a non-repetitive activity during the second period. Then he used his own words, telling his own stories, accompanying himself on the autoharp which gave him the support he needed.

Geoffrey also possessed an innate sense of form in music. In his improvisations on the chime bars or the melodica I noticed various items of eight or six bars. When he was improvising, I wrote them down as he watched to make him conscious of what he had done, and tried to make him read them and play them again from the writing. But this met with little success. The music did not seem to belong to him any more, in spite of the fact that he had given it a title, which made sense only to himself.

Improvisation on the melodica

[The Prons]

[The Plims]

Third period

Geoffrey suffered from grave problems of social integration. He was longing to be accepted and popular, and at the same time, aware that he was a 'special' boy in the school. It was important for him to be in a group, functioning as well, if not better, than the others: where he could integrate and enjoy the activities on 'equal terms' as he was doing with me already. Moreover, in any occupation, certain results can be obtained only through the dynamism of a group.

After three months of individual music therapy, I attempted some group work with Geoffrey. He had by then built up with me a stable relationship and had acquired enough instrumental skills to share the musical activities with other children and feel adequate. Within three years I made two attempts at group work, the first at the end of the third month. But after a few weeks it had to stop because of a change in the premises and could not continue. The group work was resumed a year later on the same lines but with a more serious approach, with two normal boys chosen by Geoffrey.

Geoffrey was equipped well enough to feel confident that he could play his part in the group, and even take a leading role. In the later group we added a few theoretical activities related to the form, the writing or the meaning of music, which were familiar to the boys. Their emotional outlet became musically more purposeful and orderly. Already in the first group I had tested Geoffrey's ability to bear stress and noise, to share with other children, to keep silent, to listen to others, or even to tolerate physical contact. The technique of sharing and choosing instruments with the other boys worked relatively well as it had done with me alone.

Musically, they made a successful group, operating together and simultaneously. They learnt how to make gradual changes in the music, and develop a tune purposefully. They learnt how to achieve the effects of softness and loudness, playing a thoughtful crescendo or diminuendo, a rallentando or an accelerando, or making a sudden, controlled change in speed or intensity. They learnt how to stop, to play in turn, how to listen to one another, to imitate or contradict rhythmical or melodic patterns suggested by one of them. In short, they were able to communicate through non-verbal sounds and at their own level. In the process Geoffrey did not feel that he was a 'special' boy. He worked as well as the other boys, and was accepted on musically equal terms. Some of the activities aimed at the liberation of Geoffrey's voice, which he used as a means of defence and which sometimes prevented him from revealing his own identity. I made the three boys use their unconditioned voice as it exists before being socially acceptable. The uninhibited playing of drums and cymbals and the use of movement stimulated them. They often shouted, yelled, howled or screamed without restraint, at the same time running, challenging or chasing each other round the room. It was at first a physical outlet, a preverbal experience, not even rhythmical. But the instinctive need for order prompted the boys to put some rhythm into their vocal noises. The sounds became more human and meaningful, and took on the character of a communication. I hoped that in the process Geoffrey would become conscious of his own vocal identity and give up the pathological use of his voice.

The second group was formed two years later with Geoffrey having matured in many ways and being more conscious of himself. The group of three included two other boys of the same age who were musical, imaginative and alert. The group had no relation to the music classes at school. Indeed, our activities never became a learning situation in which Geoffrey would have been disadvantaged. It opened to the boys an immensely creative activity in which Geoffrey could be musically at his best. The creative process was more important than the intellectual or cognitive processes which he could not master yet.

Each session included first a structured period needing some control or self-discipline, for instance in the playing of variations on 'Frère Jacques' on various instruments. Each of the boys in turn was put in charge of the conducting with the proper techniques, supervising and taking responsibility.

Each of the boys was able to invent his own rhythm pattern and memorise it. We wrote it down on the score. Geoffrey was the most inventive, the only difficulty being to make him keep throughout to his own pattern.

This was the area in which Geoffrey's musical gift could be used and developed without frustration. He learnt how to handle his sticks in the right way, to use his hands independently, to follow up and to keep to his own pattern. With the older boys he achieved a good musical standard of performance, and was possibly capable of improvement. They also achieved satisfactory results on five or seven-beat rhythms, mixing together the sounds of different pitched drums, of chime bars, and producing a continuo on the lower open strings of the cello. They improvised so-called 'Chinese music', or 'crazy music' on the pentatonic scale. Before playing they discussed their own name as a group and the title of

Three drummers

Played by Geoffrey and two others.

the improvisation. This followed a well-organised pattern of short passages following one another and showed that they were listening to one another. The themes were sometimes in the form of questions and answers which succeeded one another in the musical sequences. Some of the parts were humorous.

Many of the improvisations were on the theme of a story told by one of them, usually Geoffrey. The stories suggested the use of many imitative noises related to the fire brigade, a haunted house, or a storm in the jungle, produced in the most unconventional and imaginative ways on musical instruments. Drum sticks can be made to sound like the bones of a skeleton if used properly. As the boys' performance improved, I stayed away from the group and sat at the end of the room. Geoffrey was then ready to function on his own among a peer group without an adult, and feel adequate throughout the session. His trio was ready to integrate in a larger group, when such a group could be found. If, in spite of his innate musical gifts Geoffrey had not yet succeeded in the mastery of a musical instrument, at least percussion group work and his vocal ability would give him a fair chance of success in the community.

4 Parents

The cases discussed in this book have all been treated by the author for continuous periods of at least four years. None of the children was hospitalised at the time. Each of them was well cared-for at home and had one or two siblings, in a fairly normal family environment.

The inclusion of hospitalised cases would have broken the unity of a comparative study. The family environment plays an important part in the behaviour of the autistic child who is so much influenced by factors outside himself. Moreover, the family is usually much disrupted by the presence of such a child, and the hospital is not.

This is not the place to discuss the merits of family life or of hospitalisation. Music therapy can operate well with hospitalised patients. The value of music as a means of communication and projection is universal and the techniques of music therapy described in the book are applicable everywhere, provided that the music therapist is a member of the therapy team.

We have seen that the developmental process of socialisation has helped the child little by little to enlarge his musical territory enough to include first the music therapist and other people with whom he can share his music. These include his teachers, other children and his parents. This development has enabled Oliver to join a strumming group of adolescents, Geoffrey a percussion band. Martin and Pamela have learnt how to share their music with a partner; the autistic group at the clinic is enjoying moving to music together. But the influence of the parents' attitude towards music was paramount in the progress of some of the children.

Nearly all the parents, whether musical or not, were convinced that music could not be anything but 'good' for him or her, since the child seemed to enjoy it. Sometimes, at a deeper level, music created a bond between parent and child, or a bridge between them when the parent was willing or anxious to be involved. This usually happened when music had a place in the home, or when one of the parents cared for music, or even was musically educated.

The parents' attitude towards music is a factor in the quality of their relationship with the music therapist. It ranges from unwarranted hopes to a misconception of what music therapy can achieve. Most parents leave it to the specialist, a few are interested enough to ask about the music the child should have at home, others wish to participate in his musical activity, to share with him the same pleasure, and to try to provoke an active communication with him. Whatever the case may be, we have to bear in mind that the parents of an autistic child are at least as vulnerable as the child himself, irrespective of the attitude they adopt. The mother and father are frustrated parents of a frustrated child, the bewildered parents of a bewildered child, the frightened parents of a frightened child, the anxious parents of an anxious child. They sometimes interpret his behaviour as 'naughty', 'unwilling to learn to listen or to speak'. They may be little aware of or unable to resist his manipulations, or to bear his temper tantrums. The team dealing with the child, including the music therapist, has to be fully understanding and sympathetic without getting emotionally involved with the child or his parents, and be to them all someone they can trust.

The parents provide the child with an environment crucial to his general development and his behaviour. Their attitude towards food, sleep, social manners, speech and so on is helpful or harmful to him. Their attitude towards music plays a part in his reaction to music and to the effect of the therapy. Parents of a handicapped child are in need of specific help, advice and encouragement from those working with the child, the family clinic, the psychiatrist, the social worker, the teachers and the therapists. They are all involved in the process.

The following pages give several examples of how the parents can help or hinder the work of the music therapist and the inter-personal relationships which can grow between them. Quite often the parents express a rewarding gratitude to the therapist dealing with their child.

Perhaps one of the most difficult aspects of music therapist parent-relationship is the irrational hope which some parents place in music, thinking that the child may possess a great gift for music which would compensate for his learning problems. It is not easy to deal with this hope and make the parents understand where lies the real value of music to their child.

The therapist has also to form with the parents a healthy relationship of mutual trust and concern for the child. He or she has to avoid the feelings of possessiveness and jealousy which are so dangerous and harmful under the cover of love. The relationship is easier when the parents themselves are interested and become involved in the musical activities of the child.

The mother of an autistic boy or girl is a deeply deprived individual who has failed to build up a satisfactory relationship with her child. If she can relate to him at the level of a very simple musical experience, both may benefit from it. This last remark applies to the father as well.

Even when the child is not and never will be able to achieve anything, music can be an emotional link between parent and child. For example, the case of a severely autistic girl of ten suffering from grave brain damage, unable to communicate. Nevertheless, she responded to music and enjoyed the soft, relaxing sounds played to her. Her father was a professional musician and felt happy that music could reach his unfortunate child. He thought that at least he had given her a love of music and a background of beautiful sounds.

The parents' musical taste or education, the existing or non-existing amenities in the home for making or listening to music are important factors if a link is desired between home, day hospital or school where the child is cared for.

A musically discriminating father wanted to know if it were good for his boy to hear only eighteenth-century music at home, because to the parents this was the best of all music. They spoke of other kinds of music in a deprecating manner. They did not realise that their own strict and prejudiced musical preferences reflected their own strict disciplinary attitude to the child in the home. They did not consider that music should be to the boy an enlarging, not a restrictive experience. But I gave him all the liberation and freedom he could get from music, even in accepting the deliberate mistakes he made against the rules (p. 103) and his imitation of pop singers.

Other parents realise the value of music to their child. Some of them buy stereo equipment and records, so that they can listen with the child to the music he likes; This was done successfully by the parents of a boy of fifteen coming out of autism. Parents such as these do not expect more than the child can achieve, but understand what he can gain from music.

In many homes where the child's behaviour is disturbing, the child is put in front of a television or radio set and left to indulge in long sessions during which he keeps quiet, but becomes hypnotised and escapes more and more in an unreachable world of his own. The process is far from beneficial and the therapist has to help the child regain his spontaneous reactions to music.

Any interest the parents show in the child's musical experience creates a bond and gives a support which is beneficial to them all. So it was with the father who drove a long way to bring the child to music therapy sessions and to be present himself (p. 47). It was a long drive which they both enjoyed. A parent who attends the sessions can discuss the child's problems and his behaviour at home, his progress or regressions closely linked with music therapy. The image a mother has of her autistic child can be altered when she attends a well conducted music therapy session, where she sees her child becoming more communicative and better controlled, perhaps behaving almost like a normal child: he seems to enjoy himself. Her behaviour then may reveal many of her feelings about the child, her anxiety, her fright of tantrums, her desire to spoil him, her frustration or her sense of guilt. She is often then ready to receive advice or guidance. A musical climate can help the mother to open up, as it does to the child. This happened to the mother of a very disturbed boy when she saw him looking happy and more controlled than at home. She told the therapist at the third session: 'I wish his daddy could come and see him here'. She herself observed and learnt much from the therapist's quiet and patient handling of the child. After a while she believed that music had made a miraculous effect on the boy and that he had almost become 'a good boy'. In reality the mother had begun to accept the child as he was, to handle him better and to relate to him, because of what the music sessions had revealed to her. At home the boy was encouraged to dance with his little sister as he did with the therapist. He also played on a set of chime bars with his mother, as he had done during the music session.

If, as often happens during a music therapy session, the child throws things about, the mother attending the session will probably pick them up herself although the therapist has told the child to pick them up. The demand usually provokes violent manipulative behaviour from him. The situation is a well-known one at home. Little by little the mother learns that she should not pick up the objects if, like the therapist, she doesn't accept being manipulated.

It sometimes happens that an autistic child is born to parents of superior intelligence. Autism destroys the image they had formed before his birth, of a child who would benefit from a cultured environment and carry on their intellectual pursuits. Their hope to give him a superior education is deeply frustrated, although they may not reject him.

In the following case, the mother was courageous, intelligent and musical. She had dreamt of opening to her child the world of culture to which she herself belonged. The boy, her first born six-year-old child was autistic, passive and withdrawn. When it was decided he should do music, we gave her the opportunity she was longing for, namely to develop herself the child's mind and emotions.

The boy seemed to react well to music in spite of his passivity and his negativism. But the family lived too far from London for the small boy to be brought to town often enough, and there was then no music therapist in the region. It was decided that the boy would visit the music therapist from time to time with his mother, but that she would come herself regularly, be taught what to do next and report on the boy's progress week after week.

This approach could certainly not be called music therapy, but under expert guidance it was a satisfactory substitute. It helped a very deprived mother to build up a good musical and personal relationship with the child. He was able to acquire a small musical knowledge which helped him when he entered a ESN school at a later stage.

At first she tried to base the activities on a teaching-learning situation, but discovered that music had a different meaning to an autistic child. It influenced his behaviour towards her as the provider of music. He followed her about the house asking for music. She also observed that his fits of screaming were disappearing, and he showed some sign of independence.

He also developed some ability to sing, to use the chime bars and the drums, absorbing some rudiments of music as well as he could. The results were satisfactory and gratifying to the mother. She played to him the only music she could relate to, namely eighteenth-century music. She avoided emotional romantic music. I thought that we could experiment with making the child listen to music of a colourful, evocative, flowing kind. We tried *Vltava* by Smetana. The result was immediate and striking. She wrote:

'It is the most moving thing to observe his passionate love of it. He has only to hear the first notes to stop dead in whatever he is doing and comes to sit absolutely still, wrapped in the sounds. It is already the music he likes best.'

Many changes were taking place around the boy. The mother had passionately wanted another child. Now she was pregnant, full of hopes and anxiety. Although the boy seemed to be undisturbed, she reported a drastic change in his reaction to the Smetana, which she could not explain. She wrote a few weeks later: 'He seems to be worried at the part when the river rushes violently through the rapids. He quite often buries his head in my lap or puts his fingers in his ears and takes them out when the music is quiet again.'

Later on she wrote: 'I can no longer play the Smetana to him. He is disturbed not only by the crescendo but by the main theme, putting his fingers to his ears and hiding his head in my lap.'

Even if one could make an analytical study of the boy's new reaction, the approach could not have been called music therapy. But the shared educational activities had enabled the mother to build up a unique relationship with her autistic child through various musical means. She herself deplored the scarcity of music therapists in her area. Nevertheless the musical skills the boy had acquired enabled him to participate in the enjoyable family music-making group. Later on he went to a residential centre. The mother herself had immensely benefited from the experience. Not only had she found in music an incomparable means of communication with her son, but the experience prompted her to study music herself and to find in it later on a source of strength and inspiration throughout a very difficult life.

The smallest musical achievement of an autistic child is best measured in terms of human satisfaction rather than musical results. It was a proud day for the mother of an autistic boy to announce at a parents' meeting that 'John can play the piano and read music.' The performance was a five-note tune, the result of two years' work – but what had been achieved could not be measured by any normal standards. But even when the parents are not musical, and are not personally involved, they can measure the value of music in the pleasure the child experiences and the beneficial changes in his behaviour. When the parents are musical and not frustrated by the level of achievement, they can assess its value. This is what Pamela's father said:

'Music therapy as I saw it applied by Miss Juliette Alvin on my own autistic daughter was initially a controlled stimulation, then the means of opening a door to senses before then untapped, thereby reaching levels of intelligence and provoking responses which enabled the therapist to offer greater challenges of performing and understanding to an hitherto underperforming child. Then, not to forget a most important aspect, the child thoroughly enjoyed doing it.'

5   A new challenge

In September 1984 I began a new venture which was to prove a tremendous challenge to my development as a therapist. Until this time, my experience of autistic children had been in a hospital school where the children had severe learning difficulties in addition to the autistic state. This necessitated a more behavioural approach, particularly in the management of self-injurious behaviour. I had to adapt my aims and objectives; e.g. music therapy might be effective in reducing the frequency of head-banging, although the expression and sharing of feelings remained at the centre of the therapy.

Juliette Alvin had worked in the Chinnor Resource Unit for three years, during which time she made a strong musical and personal impact on the children and staff. When it became possible for me to make a change in the schools I visited regularly, I was warmly welcomed to continue a therapeutic input which was valued. The work of the unit is becoming well known, nationally and internationally. It receives a large number of visitors who are attracted by its philosophy and methods of work. In addition to the educational programme, it gives the children access to a variety of therapies: Waldon, holding, music, drama and, where relevant, psychotherapy.

The unit has three bases: Chinnor (primary), Thame (secondary), and Oxford (primary, middle and secondary). The bases are situated in mainstream schools so that, wherever feasible, the children can follow a programme of integration, with support, into mainstream education. The strength of the unit lies in its philosophy of the coexistence of education and therapy. It is forward-thinking and might be considered controversial by some. The philosophy is also pragmatical with a bias towards being more psychodynamic than behavioural. What might work for individual children is tried, tested and evaluated. The involvement of parents is vital and there is an open door for them to come and discuss problems of education, management and family. Teachers and helpers are also prepared to go into the family home. The approach by staff to the children is at as low a level of intrusion as possible. This is so that the level of anxiety is not increased unduly. All staff are well prepared in the aims for each child. They are required to be flexible, imaginative and calm, yet firm in dealing with the children, who reveal a wide range of autistic features, from mild to severe. But their learning difficulties are, in general, not as profound as those I had worked with in the hospital school.

It was after beginning work in the unit that I came to be involved in a new research project including the mothers as well as the children. I was invited by Dr John Richer, Principal Clinical Psychologist in the paediatrics department of the John Radcliffe Hospital in Oxford, to give a video-illustrated talk to a professional group. He knew the children concerned as he acts in a consultative capacity to the unit. His main comment, which impressed me afterwards, was that he had noted some lovely examples of communication between each child and me: what a pity that the duo could not become a trio, so that mother might share in a special kind of communication. A similar thought had occurred to me, particularly with the increasing interest in family therapy. But I had discounted the idea as not being possible in the educational setting: I was employed by the education authority, not the health authority. However, circumstances decreed otherwise. A psychologist, Pierrette Müller, whom I had met in the course of previous work which she had observed, expressed great interest, and after consultation with professionals, including Dr Richer and parents, the research was set to proceed. Mrs Müller would use the study for a Ph.D. It began in September 1986 and ended in June 1987.

In choosing the children who would take part, we had to ensure that they fulfilled the four main criteria outlined by Michael Rutter in his definition of childhood autism. They are (1) an onset before the age of 30 months; (2) impaired social development; (3) delayed and deviant language development and (4) stereotyped behaviour patterns, such as spinning objects or flapping the hands in front of a source of light. There is also strong resistance to change in routine. Within the boundaries of this definition, our children ranged from mild to severe autism.

From my experience of children severely affected, I found the ethological approach – observing how the child behaves – very helpful. This has been well documented by both Tinbergen and, later, John Richer. I was particularly interested in the concept of the approach/withdraw behaviour of the autistic child. The avoidance of social interactions can be clearly observed. It may be by turning away when approached, or looking beyond the approaching person rather than at him. If an over-intrusive gesture is made, the child will move away. When the autistic child is in a state of conflict, a moving towards a person or object followed by moving away can be seen in an alternating pattern. I noticed this on a number of occasions when a new instrument was in the room. It was important that the child was given enough space to discover it in his or her own time. I often saw the approaching/withdrawing behaviour until the child decided that it was safe to explore the instrument by touching it and eventually producing sounds. This was one aspect which Mrs Müller was interested to measure as part of her analysis of the project.

She decided to incorporate four hypotheses to be investigated.

1 Music therapy shows some positive effects in autistic children.
2 The effects will generalise into everyday life.
3 The mother's involvement will help the generalisation.
4 The mother's perception of and attitude towards her child will become more positive so helping to build communication, through sound and music, as the communication begins at the child's level.

Ten children, divided into two groups, began the programme, with nine completing the research period of twenty to twenty-two sessions. Twenty was the set number but where special intervention was necessary, the number was extended to twenty-two. There were two main ten-session blocks, coinciding with the first two terms of the school year. Each music therapy session lasted approximately twenty to twenty-five minutes and took place on a weekly basis. For the first ten weeks, Group 1 received therapy without mother present, while Group 2 included mother. At the beginning of the second block of sessions, the two groups 'crossed over' so that Group 1 had therapy with mother and Group 2 without. We worked in the family home so that a consistent environment could be maintained with both mother and child feeling secure in a familiar environment. All the sessions were recorded on video.

As Mrs Müller aimed to look at the carry-over effects before and after music therapy, mothers were invited to share an activity with their children for fifteen minutes before the music session and again for fifteen minutes after. The activity might be drawing, doing puzzles, building with bricks or lego, playing games or telling stories. As long as the child was kept in the room, it did not matter whether he or she was always active or not.

Parents were involved in completing sets of questionnaires before the project started, in the middle at the cross-over point and again at the end. They included questions about how the parents would define music therapy and what their expectations of it were for their children. We did receive one or two queries as to why mothers were being involved and not fathers. It was purely a practical consideration. We could not use a parent who was out at work all day as that was the only time during which we had to work. The co-operation of the two schools, the resource unit and the hospital school (now closed), was very supportive and, in turn, we tried not to disrupt the child's school day too much. Sessions were arranged for early in the morning at the beginning of the school day, during lunchtime and after school.

This has been my only experience of a dual partnership: one between child, mother and me; and the other with the research psychologist who was always present operating the camera. Both Mrs Müller and I felt very vulnerable at first going into the family home. We had to be accepted into that environment. For the relationships to be profitable, we had to form a strong bond of trust and respect. For this reason alone, taking part in such a project was very valuable. I was no longer on my own home ground as I had been in the schools and so I could not make the glib criticisms and judgements that it is all too easy for professionals to make when they have no practical knowledge of the home circumstances. I had to learn and understand the varying dynamics encountered in each family home and adjust to them.

The aims of the researcher and the therapist had to be

mutually respected as much as possible. The therapist's aims included being actively involved, making the therapeutic aims clear, giving feedback and advice if necessary and being flexible, taking the needs of child and mother into account. The researcher's aims were to be neutral, to keep to the same routine, avoiding change and to be as unobtrusive as possible. The partnership worked well and I felt that I had quiet support when I needed it and an ear that would listen.

I had more initial misgivings about the child/mother/therapist partnership. To the best of my knowledge, involving mothers as actively as possible in the music therapy and presenting them with the opportunity to become a co-therapist had not been tried under research conditions. I was concerned about how I would involve mother. How directive should I be without inhibiting her natural response to her child and how would I cope with a response that I might feel was restrictive for the child? I wanted mother to feel as comfortable as she could within a musical situation where she might feel at a disadvantage through lack of any musical training. I had to be careful not to undermine her confidence. The children would not be a problem. I was used to working with them and some of the research group had already had individual music therapy with me in their schools.

The children who had had music therapy would have to adapt to an altered approach when mother was involved in the therapy session. They would have to learn to share their musical experiences with their mothers as well as with me. My preferred instrument for supporting the child's improvisation – the piano – could not be used. As only two of the homes had a piano, I decided to use the guitar as my main supporting instrument. Other instruments used were a large cymbal on a stand, a set of bongo drums, which could also be placed on a stand, an alto xylophone, a soprano glockenspiel and a selection of smaller hand-held untuned percussion instruments.

Once the project was under way, I anticipated that the degree of involvement on the part of the mothers would depend on how confident they felt, and the willingness to give it a try. I began to understand just how vulnerable the mothers were and how great their anxieties about their families. They needed therapeutic support as much as their children did and often I wished I could have mother on her own for a series of sessions. It became obvious that some of the mothers were holding back their own feelings in deference to those of their children. It was difficult for them to answer their child's musical challenges on the child's chosen dynamic level, i.e. very loud. A quiet, placatory responding phrase often had the opposite effect from the one intended.

By the time we were well in to the second block of sessions, it seemed that the eight mothers taking part – one mother had two similarly afflicted boys – divided into three broad categories:

1. Those who were at ease in relating to their children using sounds and music as the medium.
2. Those who had specific problems in relating to the children such as the instance given above. Each of these women needed confidence-building and permission to express how she really felt – that here was a clinical situation in which she could release the anger and frustration of having to cope with someone who could not relate in the same ways as normal children.
3. Those who for a variety of reasons – the most common being acute anxiety – were over-intrusive and concerned that the children should always be actively participating. Consequently, the children were not allowed time and space in which they could respond.

Given time, the mothers in the second category did develop more confidence and became more assertive. A more vital issue was raised by the mothers in the third category. Direct intervention was necessary. It was decided by the researcher, her supervisors and me to give them three simple instructions at the beginning of each succeeding session:

1. Avoid eye contact with the child.
2. Do not touch the child unless he or she comes to you spontaneously.
3. Avoid any physical attempt to involve the child – it does not matter if there is not active participation all the time.

The mothers concerned were intelligent. They could understand the directions on an intellectual level but because of their strong emotional involvement they found it almost impossible to carry out the directions. The dilemma for us was that the programme was drawing to a close and I realized that I could not undermine them in this delicate situation. They were also aware of the all-seeing eye of the video camera. I decided that, considering the lack of time and the rigidity of research conditions, there was little I could do. Fortunately, one of the mothers asked if she could continue with her son after the research period was over, and, given time to realize and understand her own feelings and responses in the therapy session, the problem has come to a positive resolution.

The number of sessions was too short a span of time to see real progress in most cases. I say this regardless of whatever the results of the research, still under analysis at the time of writing, may reveal. Where the autistic state is more severe, progress has to be measured in terms of years rather than months. Three of the mothers wanted to continue with their children at home. Careful planning of school timetables permitted this as, once the research was ended, I returned to working in the schools. With the absence of both the video camera and the confines of research, mother, child and I all experienced a greater sense of freedom and more space, both physical and psychological. We felt that the therapy could now grow and work. Nevertheless, some strong relationships with the mothers were established during the research period. We were able to gain from each other in sharing, communication and in understanding.

6   Case study one

The early years

Sarah is Anne and Mark's elder daughter. Her birth was a forceps delivery following a straightforward pregnancy. However, Anne was admitted to hospital a week before the birth as it was suspected that she might have diabetes. Although the tests proved to be negative, it was decided that she should be induced a day before the baby was due. The birth was a long process during which Anne became very tired but as she had heard of longer deliveries, she was not worried. She believed she had a perfect baby – until Sarah was eight months old. Sarah was born with a squint and when Anne took her back to her doctor she was referred to the paediatrician. His concern was not so much for her eyes – that could be dealt with at a later date – as for her lack of normal baby development. He asked them to return in three months. Anne and Mark were deeply shocked by this. They believed their daughter to be normal as she was so contented. She did not scream and was happy lying on her tummy looking at her hands. Because of Sarah's squint, her parents found it difficult to tell whether she was looking at them or not. With hindsight, Anne feels that her lack of experience with babies meant that she was unaware of the normal stages of development. Although she was the eldest of four children, she does not remember what her brothers and sister were like as babies. When they returned to the paediatrician, he simply stated that there was something wrong with Sarah's development but was not prepared to make any diagnosis or prognosis.

The family went to see him at six-monthly intervals. Sarah was referred to the eye clinic and she was also put under general anaesthetic twice to have her hearing tested. It was thought that perhaps she had severe hearing loss. Anne and Mark were not convinced. They knew that she could hear, but she selected what she heard. She was only interested in sounds that had special meaning or appeal for her. This was during the long and depressing period when Anne and Mark had to come to terms with the fact that their wanted child had problems. Anne had gone through her own childhood feeling that she was inadequate at school and a poor achiever, although she went on to college and qualified as a teacher. It seemed to her as though Sarah was repeating her own poor beginning which Anne resented. She felt that she was projecting her own inadequacies on to Sarah and experienced feelings of violence towards her. Anne found disciplining Sarah very difficult. She did not appear to react and, when she was a toddler, spent the whole day wandering from one drawer to another, opening them and removing the contents. Padlocks had to be fitted for safety reasons. Anne reached the point where she told the health visitor that she felt like killing her child. Both sets of grandparents lived too far away to give any real support and Anne was conscious that they, too, had to come to terms with having a less-than-perfect grandchild. No one seemed able to tell Anne and Mark what was wrong. Mark also found coping with Sarah very difficult. Although superficially he seemed to manage better than Anne in the early days, his way of coping was to distance himself physically and emotionally. He was ambitious and hard-working. It was easy for him to lose himself in work, both in his business life and in the house.

Between the ages of two and a half and three years, Sarah was taken to see a psychologist on the advice of a friend who was in the medical profession. He was positive and told them not to worry. But Anne was very depressed. Everyone else's children of the same age were talking and learning to play. Sarah was not doing either. Louise, her younger sister was born when Sarah was two and a half. Eventually, the health visitor found a playschool which was the equivalent of an opportunity play-group, a group for children with learning difficulties. For the first time, Sarah was accepted as she was, whereas she stood out as being different in the local village playschool.

When the family moved to a different area, an opportunity playgroup was found for Sarah to attend. Her fifth birthday, the age when she would need to start school, was approaching and it was at the playgroup that she was seen by the educational psychologist. He was sympathetic and positive but was not in a position to make any diagnosis. He recommended that Sarah should go to a purpose-built nursery school with a welfare assistant. Here, Sarah began to make real progress. Speech had begun to develop and she was able to have speech therapy. She was also beginning to relate to others and learning to play. She remained in the nursery school until she was six when the psychologist found a place for her in a local special school where the headmaster observed her very carefully for the first two weeks. He invited Anne and Mark to see him as he was concerned that the placement was not right for Sarah. However, he had been making enquiries and thought he had found somewhere suitable – the Chinnor Resource Unit. They visited the unit, where it was suggested that they should see Dr John Richer in Oxford. For the first time, they were able to discuss their problems with someone who understood exactly what they were telling him. He was familiar with the behaviour Sarah was exhibiting and was able to give positive and practical advice in how to cope, the first they had received. Chinnor could offer Sarah what she needed – assessment and support of her needs and the opportunity to mix and learn with her normal peer group when she was ready. Anne was able to meet the mothers of the other children in the unit; women who were experiencing very similar problems. They were mothers of autistic children.

As the family did not live in Oxfordshire, there was some delay while they waited for their own education authority to agree to send Sarah over the county boundary for her special schooling. The agreement was made and Sarah began at Chinnor when she was six and a half. Her progress became more consistent with the specialist help she was able to have. From simply asking for things she wanted, she was eventually able to hold a conversation. Her awareness increased to the extent that she understood that she had difficulties and there were times when she was a very sad child. Sarah realized that it was normal to make friends and was anxious to have them. However, she had little idea of how to approach others of her own age, to make friends or to sustain a friendship. These problems remain to the present day.

Sarah was referred to me for individual music therapy sessions in 1984, when she was eight. She loved music and whenever there was music in the school, whether in the unit, the school assembly, or school concerts, Sarah became absorbed. However, this was not a justifiable reason for her having music therapy. The referral was made on the grounds that she had such difficulties in making relationships that a one made through music might generalize into other areas. She also needed a medium in which she could express herself without the limitations of her understanding of language. When one first meets Sarah, it is easy to believe that her level of comprehension is higher than it actually is because of her comparatively good ability to read and to express herself. Some of her language is learned response, not necessarily properly understood. At the same time, she can have flashes of perception which are disconcerting when one knows her well.

Music therapy
During her first therapy session, Sarah, a pretty, brown-haired, blue-eyed girl, was quiet. She was not prepared to talk to me very much. However, she was more forthcoming in communicating with me using the instruments. There was sensitivity to changing dynamics between loud and soft as well as an instinctive feeling for structure and phrase length. As the sessions progressed, Sarah lost her initial shyness, revealing a strong personality that was determined to have its own way and that was skilful in manipulation of adults in order to do so. She enjoyed turn-taking and was able to pick up and use any musical cues I gave her. When her shyness disappeared, Sarah used her very true singing voice spontaneously and she enjoyed our frequent improvised recitatives. Her sense of rhythm was excellent and it was when she was beating the untuned percussion instruments such as the bongo drums that some of her inner conflicts began to be revealed. There were times when she asked that we should play quiet, slow beats, but she could only sustain this for a very short time before she would make either a rapid accelerando or a sudden dramatic change to powerful and frenzied beating. Her facial expression changed to what I could only interpret as fearful glee. This pent-up inner energy needed to be channelled. Music therapy was one way but as time went on, I became

convinced that it should not be the only way. Her weekly sessions would not be enough.

During the following year, the unit introduced supervised and supported group sessions of holding therapy. Sarah and Anne were part of the group. In this form of therapy, the mother (or father) is directly stopping the child from avoiding. It is highly intrusive with bodily contact and face-to-face interaction, offering the possibility for communication of feelings of both parent and child within a supportive and loving environment. The child can change from avoiding to anger followed by a resolution where the child can become relaxed and cuddles into the parent. When the research project ended, I became a supporter for Sarah and Anne in the holding sessions. This gave me the opportunity to observe what was happening but, even more important, it has given an added dimension to my relationship with Anne and Sarah. Holding has helped but it is still not enough.

When the music therapy research commenced, Anne and Sarah were in the group where both were taking part in the therapy during the first block of sessions. Anne showed herself to be a willing participant as she was aware how much music meant to Sarah. As Sarah had had music therapy for two years, she was in a position of superiority. She was familiar with the format of the sessions and found it difficult to understand that her mother would have to learn how to use the medium of music in a way that she had never experienced before, i.e. spontaneous improvising. With practice, and despite Sarah's occasional criticisms, Anne improved her skills on the melodic instruments. She had no problems with the drums, cymbal or tambour, those instruments essentially used for pulse and rhythms, and she enjoyed singing.

As the sessions progressed, Sarah's attempts to manipulate Anne and, to a lesser extent, me, were more apparent. The most challenging session was the fifth. Anne was suffering from premenstrual tension and a bad cold. Sarah, aware that her mother was not herself, was determined to establish herself as the dominant member of the trio. Her mood was approaching manic; she was restless and found it difficult to cope with her body when sitting on the floor from where we worked. Before we started playing, we were talking about imitation or 'copying' which was an easier term for Sarah to understand. She became obsessed with the idea, often insisting during the course of the session that we should always copy what she did. I tried to make it clear that we would copy her if we felt like it. Otherwise we would play and sing as we wanted to. She might even like to copy us. She chose not to accept this.

The session opened with a long greeting sequence: hello; hello, everyone; how are you today? Sarah chose the glockenspiel while Anne had the alto xylophone – the two instruments were side by side. They were tuned to the pentatonic scale: C, D, F, G, A. I sang and played a short melodic motif for 'Hello, everyone,' on Sarah's glockenspiel, which she watched and imitated immediately, playing and singing it. Anne repeated it on the xylophone. Sarah's attention was captured by this motif and she played it at intervals throughout the session. Musically, this opening sequence was very interactive between the three of us. I continued by singing improvised phrases about the weather outside – it was raining. Anne accompanied me, playing gentle glissandi up and down the xylophone. Sarah provided contrast by playing my rhythm on the glockenspiel briefly before imitating Anne's glissandi. This was a moment of musical symbiosis for them.

As the session continued, Sarah began to make more musical and verbal demands. She wanted us only to copy her. I was prepared to compromise but made it clear when I was resisting her demands through my music. Anne found her daughter so intrusive that she withdrew into the quiet glissandi she had played at the beginning. From time to time, Sarah began to make some aggressive hitting movements with her beater towards her mother's face which Anne chose to ignore. I directed Sarah back to the instruments – this was where she should direct any frustration with our lack of total compliance.

The final part of the session, which was entirely composed of improvisation, consisted of us playing together and changing instruments when we wanted to. Sarah's music showed an increasing number of musical outbursts where the tempo was frenetic and the dynamics much stronger. I moved the drums closer to Anne so that she could make more impact on the improvisation by playing them. I think that Sarah realized that we were not always ready to meet her demands and so she tried another ploy – verbally directing us when to stop and when to start again. Anne and I tacitly agreed to follow her. Some strong, swinging, rhythmic sequences resulted. This improvisation ended with a loud climax together, followed by a short silence.

I began to sing, 'Now it's nearly time for us to stop.' Sarah interrupted me by singing, 'That's the goodbye song,' after a short outburst on the tambour and tambourine which were either side of her on the floor. I sang goodbye to Anne. Sarah sang a loud 'Goodbye, bang' with another hitting movement towards her mother. I continued. Sarah looked at me and announced that I was to copy her. I sang, 'Why?' and she sang in reply, 'because I want you to.' The recitative continued with my insisting it was time to sing goodbye. The session had to end. Sarah retaliated by playing and singing the 'Hello, everyone' motif on the glockenspiel. Anne accompanied her quietly on the xylophone. Two successive goodbyes were answered by Sarah's hellos. When I suggested that she should sing goodbye to her mother, Sarah responded with a rapid outburst on the tambour and tambourine. When I insisted, Sarah turned swiftly to her mother, singing, 'Goodbye, bang,' and hit her across the cheek. Sarah became very frightened at her mother's spontaneous tears and hastily said she was sorry. Quietly, I asked her why she did it. She answered that she did not know and gave what has been described as the 'fear grin' – not a true smile but a stretching of the mouth with the upper lip tight over the top teeth. She moved close to her mother, smoothed Anne's hair back from her forehead and asked her if she was sad. I asked Sarah to hold her mother – she put her arms around her, fascinated by Anne's tears. She asked, 'Why are you so sad?' Anne replied that she was sad not because Sarah had hit her but because she had wanted to. At this, I moved behind mother and daughter and held them close. Sarah began talking about discussing it during the holding session they were having the next day.

As Anne and Sarah talked and calmed themselves, it was obvious that Sarah could not fully understand the consequences of her actions. Anne explained, as I had done before on many occasions, that the instruments were there to be hit and for feelings to be expressed while playing them, but people were not. Sarah turned to me and asked whether I was angry with her. I was not, although I was angry at what she had done. I reiterated that the instruments were there so that she and Anne could show how they felt. If we were angry with her, we could express it through our music, not by hitting her. We ended by exchanging quiet goodbyes to each other.

Following this session, I had to come to terms with my own feelings. I felt guilty that I did not prevent such a happening. Perhaps I should have been more directive. With hindsight, and after looking at the video, it would probably have happened anyway. Sarah had to understand that we were not there to bow to her wishes every time she made them known. She could not always be in control in her self-centred way. It seemed that the only way she could cope was using her unpredictable, physical aggression destructively. When she was in this extreme mood, she had to be given her own time to work through it. The unit staff had had similar experiences with her. She was also very determinedly resisting the ending of the session, not uncommon in music therapy. I also had to re-examine the degree of emotional involvement of the therapist with the clients. The therapist can only understand by being prepared to experience some of their anger and pain but at the same time being able to put it behind him or her. Because of the music therapist's active involvement in music-making with the client, some emotional involvement is inevitable but the therapist must be able to stand back and analyse the changing relationship with compassion but not sentimentality.

In the following session, I suggested to Anne that she, too, should use the music-making to express what she felt about Sarah and me. She found it very difficult and was frightened of the possibility of losing control. She needed a great deal of support. Gradually, she did learn to be more assertive with Sarah in her music, meeting her challenges with matching tempo and dynamics. There was no repeat of the aggression of the fifth session. However, it was decided to have two extra sessions at the end of the second block so that Anne could join us again. If appropriate, after the first extra session, I would have a session with Anne on her own. It proved not to be necessary.

I decided to be more directive than usual at the beginning of session 21. During the greeting, I held the tambourine, beating it in accompaniment while I sang Hello to Anne first, then to Sarah, offering each the tambourine to play although I retained hold of it. This provoked laughter, especially when I shortened the time for exchanges, speeding up the action. As both mother and daughter were receptive, it set the prevailing mood for the session. The main part involved improvising while we moved around the instruments as we wished; which might include playing the same instrument as someone else. The moving from one instrument to another was much more positive than it had been in earlier sessions. There were occasions when Sarah tried to interrupt by talking to either one of us. Generally we ignored this and continued playing. At one point, Sarah told her mother that she hated day-dreaming. Anne suggested that she should try to put the feeling into her playing. There was a greater sense of equality between us. Sarah, who was only too happy to invade our instrumental territories, did not object when we invaded hers. However, there was an exception near the end of the improvisation when Anne was playing on the glockenspiel with Sarah and I began to beat the tambour which was lying on Sarah's lap. The bond of trust which had been established between Sarah and me over the preceeding two years was strong enough for me to challenge her. There was a spark of anger from her. She threatened to hit me but decided against it when both Anne and I exclaimed, 'No!' together. Then she accepted that we were playing on her instruments and began to enjoy what, for her, had been an anxious experience to begin with. We ended together with a succession of fast beats, with Sarah and Anne sharing the tambour, still on Sarah's lap. Sarah had to have the final beat and we let her.

I suggested that we should end by singing together, if we all agreed. Sarah went to collect a songbook, the cover of which attracted her. As we looked through it, she recognised 'Puff, the Magic Dragon'. We agreed to sing it, with guitar accompaniment. Sarah was reluctant to sing with us consistently throughout and so we invited her to sing on her own if she preferred. She was not very sure and tried putting on a peculiar voice. But we persuaded her, eventually, to sing in her own voice even though it was quiet. Then I introduced them to an 'echo' song; where I sang a line and they repeated it. This was highly successful and as the verses progressed, eye contact between Sarah and Anne increased. They were able to smile at each other, and in the second part of the final verse, Sarah turned to her mother, put her hands on Anne's knees and swiftly kissed her.

When it came to the exchange of goodbyes, I accompanied my goodbye by strumming across the open strings of the guitar. I handed the guitar to Sarah for her to hold, play and sing on her own before passing the guitar to Anne. Finally, I sang, 'Goodbye, everyone,' to which Anne and Sarah responded together.

This session showed how positive a resolution there could be for Sarah when she was in a receptive mood. It was heartening for Anne to share an activity with Sarah in which Sarah would allow herself to be involved and where she could shed some of the anxiety which ruled her life and prevented her from taking on new ventures. For this reason, Anne and Sarah continued the sessions in their home for a further year after the research period ended. During this year, I introduced the electronic keyboard as Sarah preferred melodic instruments. She became interested in music for its own sake and her concentration span increased as she explored chord structures and different timbres of sounds. We left her free to explore. I made no attempt to teach her, although Sarah did express a wish to learn the piano several times. But her moods were too unpredictable and her attention span too short for her to accept the more traditional methods of teaching. She was learning far more through her own improvisations where she had to rely on her acute ear. Sometimes Anne and I, in turn, played in duet with her at the keyboard or else provided rhythmic support. The emotional highs and lows continued but there was still a strengthening bond between the three of us.

The beginning of the next academic year brought a change for Sarah when she transferred to the unit's base in a nearby comprehensive school. The sessions at home had to cease but I carried on with individual therapy with Sarah. I was able to use a practice room in the music block which was not far away from the unit base. Having the use of a piano meant that the therapy could be taken on further as Sarah loved the instrument and with its great potential for range of expression we might achieve more in exploring feelings. Through the music and holding sessions, as well as the general approach by the staff of the unit, Sarah was made more aware of feelings but she was confused and frightened by them. She often needed to talk about them with us.

The music sessions, which still continue, have taken on a new dimension. We usually play in duet at the piano. I provide a structure and support in the bass while Sarah improvises in single notes and chords above. She talks about things that matter to her as we play. Usually these concern fears; fears that seem trivial to an outsider but which are real and magnified in her own mind. As I also support Sarah and Anne in the holding sessions, our relationship is no longer just a musical one. Sarah will often talk about issues that have been raised during holding. Because of her difficulties in understanding abstract concepts, emotions being among them, she rarely expresses such a concept consciously – apart from anger. More usually, she will offer a subject for improvisation such as someone falling asleep, thunder and lightning, a dance, or someone crying.

Sarah is now approaching puberty. It has become difficult for her family and those who are working with her to differentiate between her autistic features and what could be called the usual trials of adolescence. Anne often feels desperate. Mark has his business commitments and Louise, the younger daughter, has made her own school and social life. Anne and Sarah are together more on their own and Sarah has become more possessive towards her mother. There are times when her behaviour can be extreme and she has a lot of individual attention to try and help her. We cannot know what the future holds for Sarah but we must be positive. As her music therapist, I know that music will always be important and meaningful in Sarah's life.

7 Helen and Matthew

The early years

Helen and Simon were married in 1980. Both were university graduates, trained in biological sciences. They decided that they would not delay starting a family for too long and so Matthew was born in October 1982. Helen decided to give up work after about five months of her pregnancy. Although she thought little of it at the time, her work had involved working with pesticides over a period of six years. She does not know whether this had any effect on Matthew. However, she was healthy and the pregnancy was normal. Labour was long and she was given a hormone drip as well as two doses of the pain-killer, pethidine. Matthew was just under nine pounds at birth – Helen described him as 'a bouncing baby' and perfectly healthy. There was nothing to suggest any problems at all (later Helen was able to see the records), just a long labour but with no distress to the baby at birth.

As she was suffering from exhaustion, Helen spent most of the following three weeks in bed. Fortunately, Matthew was a very easy baby: he fed well (breast-fed), soon settling into a four-hourly pattern and slept almost all the time between. He sat up at five months. He smiled, and was fairly quiet although he would cry for his food. Otherwise, he was not very vocal and was content to sit in his pram or chair and watch his parents.

The first signs of trouble came when Matthew was five months of age. As he was a big baby, Helen had started him on solid food at about four months. She began to use diluted cow's milk on his rice cereal. He had stewed fruit and other fairly bland foods on the advice of the health visitor. One packet baby food which contained tomato and egg gave Matthew severe colic later the same day. When he was taken to the doctor, his parents were told that he had an ear infection and antibiotics were prescribed. There was a lull for some weeks, but between the ages of six and a half months and ten months, Matthew would not eat properly. Any upset to his stomach, whether it was hunger, eating or a bumpy car or pram ride, would cause him to whimper, which in turn became high-pitched, ear-splitting screams for two to three minutes. Then he would flop, and sit quietly before falling asleep. By the time he was ten months old, he was actually twitching, turning grey in the face with his eyes staring to one side and staying that way for a minute or so. He did not appear to lose consciousness. Since this time, Helen has been told that they were minor fits. When he began to lose weight, a referral was made to the children's clinic at the local main hospital. It was suggested that a food allergy might be the problem and a three-month milk-free diet was recommended after which milk should be reintroduced very gradually. The colic intensified during the first two weeks of the diet. Then it suddenly stopped. Matthew started eating, taking notice, staying awake more and putting on weight.

Matthew and food became quite a 'love affair' according to Helen. He began to crawl at thirteen months and walked at sixteen months. Milk was reintroduced with no ill effects, but he was allergic to eggs until he was two years old. Physical progress was rapid until he was described by his mother as a little whirlwind, climbing and performing daring balancing acts.

Helen was thankful that he was so obviously healthy – it seemed that they were back on safe ground. However, he failed his check-up with the health visitor when he was eighteen months old. He refused to co-operate in any of the hearing tests. Helen was convinced there was nothing wrong with his hearing although she had noticed that his hearing was selective. He heard such things as food being prepared, dishes rattling and the sound of cars, which he loved. When Matthew was referred to the audiology clinic, it was extremely difficult to get him to concentrate, but, with considerable patience by the staff, Matthew responded to a wide range of sounds. It was thought that his hearing was normal, but with his lack of co-operation it was difficult to make an accurate assessment. The tantrums began at the same time. Matthew was also eating strange things which other children of the same age had given up – woodlice were a speciality. He loved movement of any kind: playing on a swing, or riding in his pushchair, car or wheelbarrow.

By the age of eighteen to twenty-four months, Matthew had made no attempt to speak. The paediatrician was cautious. He felt the child's development was delayed and that he would like to keep him under observation. The family was asked to return in three months' time and again in six months. Taking him to the local toddler group proved disastrous – a screaming tantrum was the result each time. Visits to understanding friends' homes were more successful but it was noticed that he hated any kind of physical contact. He was no longer a cuddly child.

Helen and Simon took Matthew privately to a consultant psychiatrist, a family acquaintance, who agreed, although mental handicap was not his field, that development was delayed and if Matthew showed no improvement by the age of three years, they must seek help. At this time, a second son, Richard was born. Matthew took a long time to adjust to the new member of the family.

He was referred to a child development centre. At last, positive help was offered. It was a relief to Helen and Simon to find somewhere where there were other children with problems. The family was put under the guidance of a teacher-counsellor who worked in association with the centre. Helen felt much more confident when she realised that she had been doing the right sort of thing instinctively. It was the teacher-counsellor who suggested that Matthew might be mentally handicapped and who offered support to the family during the period of shock and bereavement. Helen felt as though she had lost a child and was grateful for the support of someone who combined honesty and sympathy, and who did not avoid the issues. Special education was talked about.

Matthew was two and a half years old when the diagnosis was made – that he had autistic tendencies. Helen felt relieved that at last there was a label. But it was a difficult time for both Helen and Simon. In Helen's words, 'It takes some months to adjust to the idea that your child is going to be peculiar for life, not just a few years. It's not the first time I've had something happen that made me stop short and say "why me", but it's a fruitless question; pointless, unhelpful.' At this time, Matthew's educational assessment was carried out. The papers were ready to go to the education department in July but, with the summer break, it was September before an acknowledgement came. It proved to be a long and drawn-out process. Helen and Simon felt totally unsupported. They had moved house in August. Helen reached breaking point with Matthew's screaming. She found she could not bear even looking at him during his screaming bouts and shut him in his room. Again, I quote from Helen's own words, 'I remember three horrible occasions when I kicked him – hard enough to shift him across the room . . . At this stage, I started to think, you are beginning to batter this child. And the awful thing was seeing a child who wouldn't stop screaming reduced to a shaking jelly. I'd just hit him as hard as I knew how and there wasn't a mark on him. What the hell do people do who batter their kids until they are black and blue all over . . . It was horrible because I thought, how far do you have to go?'

When Helen related this experience to the teacher-counsellor, she was advised to make an immediate and emphatic case to the education department. As she was a highly articulate woman, she did, with some effect. She had a reply within a week and three weeks later, Matthew commenced in the nursery class of a local special school. This had been a black period in Helen and Simon's marriage. Simon could see what living with Matthew twenty-four hours of the day was doing to Helen and resented the child bitterly. He was prepared to change, bath and feed Matthew if he had to but would not attempt to communicate or bond with him. His own growing up had not been easy and having a normal family and home of his own meant everything to him. Matthew's schooling provided the break and support that the family needed so desperately at that time.

Not long after this, the clinical psychologist who was observing Matthew heard about our proposed music therapy research and suggested that he and Helen could benefit from taking part. Helen was in whole-hearted agreement. Music was important to the family and a natural part of their lives. Helen had learnt the piano and enjoyed singing. Matthew was sung to from babyhood when it was obvious to his mother that it could soothe and relax him.

Music therapy

Matthew, an attractive, dark-haired, dark-eyed child began his music therapy sessions in September 1986, when he was three years, eleven months old. For the first block of ten sessions, he had music therapy alone with me. During the first few sessions, I hoped that we could find and meet each other musically so that a relationship of trust and enjoyment could grow; where Matthew could learn that sharing and giving and taking from each other was fun in a safe environment.

During the first session, Matthew was given the freedom to play the piper's tune. I would follow. We worked in the children's bedroom which was spacious enough to take the equipment. So that I would be closer to his level physically, I chose to work on the floor, an approach we have continued with as general practice until the present time. I began by opening the guitar case and strumming across the open strings of the guitar, inviting Matthew to come and look. I sang his name and then, 'Hello, Matthew.' He stood still and watched me. I took the guitar out of the case and played and sang, 'Hello, Matthew,' a number of times, leaving silences between the phrases so that he could respond in any way if he wanted to. He decided to come closer and ran his fingers down the strings, gently at first, then more energetically. As he did so, I sang 'Baa, baa, black sheep' to his strummed accompaniment. When I put the guitar back in its case, Matthew followed my movements, with his face close to the guitar.

I picked up the bongo drums and placed them on the floor. Matthew turned them over and fiddled with the wing nut inside. When I turned the drum right side up again and lightly tapped it with my fingers, Matthew ran off to hide by a cupboard. I beat and sang,.'Matthew, where are you?' He peered out. I picked up the sleigh bells and the maraca. He came out of his hiding place and took the bells from me. I improvised on the phrase, 'Matthew has the bells,' accompanying him on the bongo drums. 'Matthew can make the bells ring,' was interrupted by his first vocal responses, 'ah ya', and sometimes 'oy yoy', which I imitated and extended into slightly longer musical phrases.

Still holding the bells, Matthew jumped on to his bed. I continued to vocalise, shaking the maraca in accompaniment and time to his bouncing. I carried on improvising on 'Matthew is bouncing on the bed,' changing the accompanying instrument to the tambour. This evoked no response from him. I took the bells which he had discarded and shook them high above him – by this time he was lying down. He reached up for them. Again I accompanied his occasional shaking of the bells and his bouncing by singing and beating the tambour. When I offered him the maraca, he took it, but decided that he did not want to play with it. Bouncing was more stimulating.

As he continued, I took the guitar again and sang, 'Matthew, that's your name. Matthew is dressed in blue.' From time to time, Matthew stopped to watch what I was doing. When I offered him the guitar to strum, he made a brief vocal response; a very abrupt sound. When I vocalised, he did not respond. Matthew reached over with his feet, placed them on the guitar, including the strings. Then he hid his head under a blanket. I began to sing, 'It's nearly time to stop.' He picked up the bells and dropped them on to the floor. I repeated that it was nearly time to go – and to sing goodbye. Matthew responded with a short crying sound. I sang a series of goodbyes to him and 'Goodbye, guitar,' as I put it in the case. As I sang, I strummed across the open strings as I had at the beginning of the session. Then I took Matthew by the hand, and led him to the case before I closed it. He watched as the lid was lowered gently, again holding his face close to it.

There were clear indicators from this session. These included some positive responses even though they were at a very infantile level. Musical sounds could distract him but his attention span was fleeting. It was going to be a challenge to take and develop those responses into interactive music-making. For this to happen, Matthew's attention would have to be captured for long enough to motivate and develop his concentration. He was a child who seemed very dependent on his own inner world, and who showed little interest, apart from the necessitites of life, in being part of the world of family and home around him.

Over successive sessions, Matthew made more approaches and his vocal responses increased. It became obvious that he had a good musical ear since his responses were vocalised in whatever key I happened to be playing, whether it was on the guitar or the little soprano glockenspiel. Before the final session of the block where Matthew and I were alone together, Helen reported that it had not been a good week. He had gone 'over the top' for no apparent reason and she was concerned that the good phase of the previous three months might be over. During that tenth session, I found Matthew restless. He often giggled, which seemed to be blocking communication rather than enhancing it. The glockenspiel elicited the most response from him. Often he came near to watch and listen as I played. At one point, he even picked up the two small beaters and laid them across the bars of the glockenspiel. We were able to hold eye contact at the end of a phrase – this was a major step forward. There were a number of bed-bouncing episodes but none lasted long; all part of the restless activity. Matthew's strongest reaction came at the end of the session during the preparation for, and during, the goodbye section. I was using the bongo drums on their stand as accompaniment for 'Now it's nearly time to say goodbye,' when Matthew, who had been standing still and listening, went to the cymbal, touched it, then climbed on to the low table where some of the smaller instruments were in their box. He climbed down again and shouted. He jumped about and went to grab the microphone which I rescued. Matthew became very agitated, running to the window and climbing on to the window-sill. I approached him, holding and playing the glockenspiel. He became quiet and held eye contact briefly. Again he cried, and I lifted him down and carried him over to the guitar in its open case. I strummed. He resisted being held and I let him go. Gradually he quietened as he listened before deciding that he would join me. Once, he sighed; then I heard some chuckles. I suggested that we closed the lid of the case together. There was another single shout. He sat opposite me as I fastened the catches. Then he became disturbed, pulling at the case and pushing it across the floor. He did not like me dismantling the cymbal and insisted that it should go back on its stand by trying to do it himself. I sang some final goodbyes to him but I had to be firm, explaining that the session had ended.

It was at about this time that Helen told us that she was pregnant and that the new baby was due in July 1987. The second block of sessions which would include her with Matthew began in January. When we reappeared after the Christmas break, Matthew accepted us as a matter of course. He was in an amicable mood. I suggested to Helen that she should join in when she felt comfortable to do so, or when I made a deliberate move to involve her. My method of working with Matthew would remain as it had been; i.e. as unintrusive and non-directive as possible. Helen sat quietly on the floor near me when I began the session, as usual, by opening the guitar case, strumming the strings of the guitar and singing Matthew's name. He was momentarily distracted by the cymbal on its stand, but as I continued singing and playing, leaving silences for any responses he might want to make, he returned to the guitar and watched. He retreated to his bed. I followed him with the guitar and suggested we do a 'Hello' for mummy together. He strummed and I sang to Helen before he began bouncing on the bed. Helen sang her response and reached out to touch him. Matthew took no notice but continued to bounce with his back to us, squealing excitedly. On her own initiative, Helen sang his name. I felt her voice sounded sad. She reached for him again to prompt him to turn around, but he did so before she could touch him. He strummed again and I suggested that mummy should have a turn. As she strummed, Matthew stopped to look and listen. He moved away again but as she carried on, he came closer so that she could circle him with her arm and draw him on to her lap. He did not resist and there were some companiable moments while they strummed in turn as I held the guitar.

Another brief period of communication occurred when Matthew was sitting on the low table and Helen was playing the glockenspiel. Matthew slid to the floor, inclining his body towards the sounds. When she stopped, he gave a short sigh and brought his face close to his mother's so that they were nearly touching. Helen settled him on her lap. He did not appear to resist when she placed the beater in his hand with her hand firmly around his, guiding his playing on the glockenspiel. When she took her hand away after playing a sweeping glissando along the length of the instrument, Matthew was able to continue briefly on his own before stopping and moving away, still clutching the beater.

Soon after this, I played 'Rock-a-bye Baby'. Matthew had

moved nearer the window, but at the first line, he stood still, listened, came back, and sat on the floor nearby. Helen carried on singing when I stopped. She reminded her son that she had sung him to sleep with that song when he was a baby. Helen then played the first line on the glockenspiel and she and I hummed the remainder of the song together. A few minutes later in the session, Matthew vocalised a close approximation of the first line. Although his concentration span was so limited, he was still musically aware.

Later in the session, Helen guided Matthew's hand, holding the beater on the cymbal. As he had on the glockenspiel, he was able, with the impetus of the guided movement, to continue on his own for some more beats. When it came to the goodbye section, mother and son strummed the guitar together although in this instance, Helen was perhaps too intrusive. Matthew did not need guidance any more. He made it clear when he wanted to get up and go, patting the cymbal with his hand as he did so.

My reflections on this first session of the 'trio' involved a coming-to-terms with the differing approaches of the therapist and the mother: the therapist with the more objective view of what was happening and the mother with her emotional involvement of four years, coping with a difficult child. Helen was much more directive than I wanted to be. Sometimes it worked well, but as well as the direction, there needed to be spaces for Matthew to move away and be free if he felt he needed to. I had worked with him long enough to know that his need to respond to music was real and that he would return, given the motivation. But I also had to look at the problem from Helen's point of view. She was having another child and, although Matthew's younger brother, Richard, was healthy and very intelligent, she had anxieties for her unborn child. I felt that these anxieties were projected on to Matthew by her desire for him to succeed in the music sessions, which meant constant participation and much hoped for progress for him. Helen also expressed her lack of confidence in using music in such a spontaneous and improvised way, particularly on the tuned instruments. To begin with, she found it much easier playing the rhythmic instruments such as the drums, cymbal, tambour and tambourine. She began to realise how inhibiting her formal music training was.

As the sessions progressed, it became clear that my aim to involve Matthew in interactive music-making with us was going to be a long-term one. The frustrations for both Helen and me were caused by those wonderful and fleeting moments when he showed that it could be possible, but it had to be on his terms. Matthew was very manipulative. He would have liked us to go after him and retrieve him whenever he decided to move away from the activity area. This would give him the opportunity to resist even more. If we ignored him and improvised for ourselves, he returned. Gradually, Helen gained more confidence to make up her own melodic phrases on the tuned instruments rather than trying to pick out known nursery tunes.

The structure of the sessions remained the same although the range of improvising and the instruments used varied according to Matthew's mood and how much he was prepared to contribute. His vocalisations became more definitely pitched and tuneful. He has always responded more positively to the minor scale, particularly D minor, in improvisation. It was easier to interact with him vocally than it was using the instruments. Perhaps using his voice was not as threatening a means of communication as playing an instrument which was not an integral part of him but part of the outside world where he found it more difficult to cope.

As Helen's pregnancy progressed, Matthew's relationship with his mother changed. He became much more physical, wanting to climb all over her and lie across her. At the same time, so that Helen might not reach out to hold or guide him too much, I gave her the instructions to avoid eye contact and not to hold him unless he made the first approach. Emotionally she found this difficult to do. She was anxious and growing physically tired more easily. I began to intervene by indulging in more horseplay with him. He enjoyed being sung to, swung around and bounced at the same time. He allowed me to do this but had to realise that I meant it when I called a halt and introduced a quieter activity.

Towards the end of one of the final research sessions, Matthew pulled Helen nearer the door, wanting to be swung about and danced with. After a short time of accompanying them, I joined them and took his hand. His reaction was to drop his mother's hand and take my free hand. I linked mother and son's hands together again as the three of us sang and danced around in a circle, first one way and then the other. We all enjoyed this shared activity. Afterwards, Helen expressed surprise that he allowed this to happen. He had always held both hands of the person moving or dancing with him and this was the first time he had ever linked hands in a circle.

The research period ended in June. Both Helen and Simon wanted music therapy for Matthew to continue when the new term commenced in September. Their third child, Edward, was born in July. He is very like Matthew in many ways. They share a number of personality traits which Richard, the second child, did not. I found it interesting when we resumed the therapy sessions in September that Helen commented that in observing young Edward's development she realises that Matthew was autistic from the beginning. She does not believe that his autism was caused by illness. With Edward's birth, the natural anxiety was lifted. Helen became more relaxed with Matthew and the sessions contained a lot of spontaneous play using instruments and voices as the tools. Helen realized that she had been too intrusive at times and that, if Matthew was in one of his not-so-receptive moods, we could leave him alone and continue playing and singing together until he decided to join us. She felt more confident in allowing him time and space, one of the most vital principles of therapy. From his vocalisations, even when he distanced himself from us, there was listening going on. He was using that time and space.

Soon after this, we moved from working in Matthew's bedroom to the sitting-room where I could use the piano. Helen often plays to Matthew. His favourite composers had been those of the Baroque and Classical periods – Bach, Handel, Haydn and Mozart, although more recently in one of his more disturbed phases, he has responded more to Mendelssohn and Schumann. I use the piano mainly in a supporting role, but there have been occasions when Matthew has expressed anger and frustration in strong chordal clusters of notes. There have also been some instances of communicative turn-taking with both his mother and me on the piano. On one occasion, Helen used it with great effect to express her own feelings. During one session, Matthew pulled her over to the piano, obviously wanting her to play. She looked to me for direction. I suggested that she played to him. She played the first prelude in Book 1 of Bach's Forty-eight Preludes and Fugues. Matthew stood quietly beside her until half-way through, when he shouted and danced about. Helen's reaction was entirely spontaneous: she stopped, turned to look at him and played a loud and powerful discord. This really stopped him short. He gazed at her in complete surprise. The musical response expressing her anger at his rejection had far more impact than any verbal admonition.

We have been working together now for nearly four years during which there have been good and bad phases in Matthew's general and emotional development. Taking the long-term view, he is more communicative than he used to be and he has made progress at school. In the music therapy sessions, the musical interaction between Helen and Matthew, particularly when using the autoharp, the tambour, the kokoriko or the cabassa, can last for several minutes rather than seconds. Both enjoy this and often there is laughter. Matthew does need some direction but this direction is more effective when it comes from the music rather than our spoken instructions. For most of the sessions now, Helen is the therapist while my role has become that of the co-therapist.

In the future, there is much that Helen can share with Matthew through music. My visits can be reduced in frequency. This is one of the families with whom I feel a strong bond of trust and love. Such a relationship is a unique and precious one. We share the good times and the bad, the highs and the lows. I leave the final words to Helen:

After these years of music therapy, Matthew has developed a keen awareness of other people and of his surroundings, and a very close, affectionate relationship with me.

We have known for a long time that Matthew responded strongly to music. Music can reach him and affect his mood and behaviour when other things do not. Knowing this, I was very keen to participate in music therapy sessions with him. These sessions have been an opportunity, not to be missed, to share in the opening out of Matthew as a person and to develop a unique relationship with him. For Matthew, it is the one time in a busy week when he and I are alone together for an hour, sharing something which means a great deal to both of us.

On the negative side, it is an added burden on the therapist, already required to be very patient, to have to cope with the expectations (music lessons?), inhibitions and misconceptions of the parent. I found my own musical training, however faulty, a real hindrance in the early stages.

I feel it is a great achievement for an autistic child to enjoy giving and receiving affection, to share a joke, and to show obvious pleasure in his family's company.'

Postscript

There can be no real conclusion to such work. To conclude means to present a definite answer and to close the actual study, a study which has taken us up to the child's adolescence. But we can make a safe evaluation of what has been achieved; of the part that music has played in the treatment or the education of some autistic children, perhaps not an essential one, but as a sometimes vital component in a complex process of growth.

Music therapy is based on an exhaustive use of everything music is made of. It begins with a simple vibration which penetrates the child's closed world, producing in him a resonance and provoking a response. The process is made up of all the forms this resonance can take, how it manifests itself, and what can be done with it under expert and understanding hands for the benefit of the child.

The responses of autistic children to a musical experience are multifarious, and so are the complex and difficult techniques leading to the development of his conscious pleasure in music.

We can evaluate and direct the different stages of the child's musical development, as described in these pages, and throughout a number of years. But we have not drawn final conclusions on something which is in essence a developmental process and can grow further and further in time within the child who will become an adult.

What music has given him is difficult to measure, and it is even more difficult to assess what the child himself has given to music, except in relative terms. Nevertheless, a long-term music therapy programme has brought a number of beneficial changes in these children's behaviour, developed their consciousness, given them a means of self-expression and creativity at a crucial moment in their life.

Bibliography

PUBLICATIONS ON MUSIC THERAPY CONTAINING
REFERENCES TO AUTISM

Juliette Alvin: *Music Therapy*, Hutchinson 1975.
Rolando O. Benenzon: *Musicoterapia y educación*, Paidos 1971.
——*Music Therapy in Child Psychosis*, Charles C. Thomas 1982.
British Society for Music Therapy: Journal and Papers.
C. Gallasch: *Musiktherapie mit autistischen Kindern*, Musik-Medizin,
   March 1977.
E. Thayer Gaston: *Music in Therapy*, Collier-Macmillan, New York
   1968.
D. E. Michel: *Music Therapy*, Ch. Thomas, Springfield, Illinois 1976.
Nordoff-Robbins: *Music Therapy for Handicapped Children*, Gollancz
   1973.
Mary Priestley: *Music Therapy in Action*, Constable 1975.
A. Wigram and R. West (eds.): *Music and the Healing Process: A
   Handbook of Music Therapy*, Carden Publications 1991.
H. Willms: *Musiktherapie mit psychotischen Erkrankungen*, G. Fisher
   1975.

PUBLICATIONS ON AUTISM CONTAINING REFERENCES TO
MUSIC

Bachrach, Moseley *et al.*: *Developmental Therapy for Young Children
   with Autistic Characteristics*, University Park Press, Baltimore 1978.
Leo Kanner: *Childhood Psychosis*, W. H. Winston and Son, Washington
   DC 1973.
Ann Lovell: *In a Summer Garment*, Secker & Warburg 1978.
——*Simple Simon* (paperback edn. of above), Lion paperbacks 1984.
Gerald O'Gorman: *The Nature of Childhood Autism*, Butterworth
   1970.
Ruttenberg, Dratman, Franknoi, Wenar: 'An instrument for evaluating
   autistic children', *Journal of the American Academy of Child
   Psychiatry*, vol. 5 no. 3, 1966.
Rutter: *Infantile Autism*, Churchill Livingstone 1971.
E. A. and N. Tinbergen: *Early Childhood Autism, an Ethological
   Approach; Advances in Ethology*, Paul Parey, Berlin-Hamburg 1972.

Lorna Wing: *Autistic Children*, Constable (2nd edn. 1975).
——*Early Childhood Autism*, Pergamon Press (2nd edn. 1976).
——and Sybil Elgar: *Teaching Autistic Children*, National Society for Autistic Children, 1969.

Index

Index compiled by John Gibson